Running on Empty:

The Irreverent Guru's Guide to
Filling Up with Mindfulness

by Shelley Pernot

True North Development Press

Austin, Texas

Published 2017
Printed in the United States of America
ISBN: 978-0-9979951-0-7
Library of Congress Control Number: 2017900340

Cover design and interior illustrations by Lisa Greenleaf.
www.lisagreenleaf.com
Interior design and formatting by Noah Adam Paperman.

The life intention builder exercise is adapted from material in the *Energy Leadership Development System* and is used with the permission of the Institute for Professional Excellence in Coaching (iPEC).

Dedication

To Donald, because every good coach needs an even greater one, and to coaches everywhere who work tirelessly to bring the light of awareness into the world one person at a time.

Contents

Introduction

"Give me your tired, your poor,

Your huddled masses yearning to breathe free,

The wretched refuse of your teeming shore.

Send these, the homeless, tempest-tossed to me,

I lift my lamp beside the golden door!"

~ Excerpt from poem by Emma Lazarus entitled "The New Colossus." It is mounted on a plaque on the Statue of Liberty standing in the harbor of New York City.

I've found that the hardest part with writing is getting started. Making up your mind that you're going to write, making that commitment, setting your intention, and then staring at the blank page on an off day for God only knows how long. Writing is an intensely vulnerable exercise. Excruciating even at times. Why do I say this? Because you have to be willing to sit with the fear that the words may never come, and even if they do, will they ever be good enough? Can they ever be good enough to communicate what really needs to be said? Felt? Understood?

But the words do come eventually, and as they do, I can feel the relief as they start to fill the empty page. The momentum takes hold, and I'm hit by one sudden burst of inspiration after another. A sense of calm and peace washes over me. When the chapter is finally finished, I often look back and think, "Now, that wasn't so hard, was it, Shelley?"

When I look back at my life over the course of the past few years, I often ask myself that same question and conclude that, no, it wasn't so hard. But in many respects where I find myself these days is also nothing short of a miracle.

I'll never forget the day I realized I hated my life. You don't forget a day like that. And it wasn't falling apart in the way of a bad after-school special. (Do you remember those? Sister Mary from my Catholic school days forced us to watch them as a not so effective means of scaring kids straight.) At least if I had fallen apart, it would have been dramatic and exciting on some level. I wasn't living on the street. I wasn't strung out on drugs. I wasn't living paycheck to paycheck. I didn't have a boyfriend that beat me (actually no real boyfriend for many years) or a debilitating illness (unless being three sizes overweight and a chain smoker counts). I hadn't lost my mind or had a nervous breakdown . . . yet.

My life looked just fine, at least on paper. Which was a big part of the problem. My life, on the outside, *looked* just fine. I got up every morning, got dressed, drove myself to the office, did my job, chatted to my colleagues, went to the bar after work with friends, came home at a reasonable hour, paid my bills, managed my commitments, got up the next day, and did it all over again. Over and over and over again. Unconsciously. Some might even say mindlessly. I was floating along in a thick, dense fog, longing and aching for something unidentifiable. I felt empty. And no matter how hard I tried, I just couldn't put my finger on what was wrong.

What was wrong was that, somewhere along the way, my spirit had died. Although of course I didn't realize it at the time. The rational side of me didn't believe in woo-woo things like a spirit that can die.

In my down time, I logically evaluated my life. Education – tick. Job – tick. House – tick. I had ticked all the boxes. Done everything "right" according to the definition of right that I had been taught. I was supposed to be happy at this point.

Happiness was supposed to have been my reward for following the rules. I was responsible. Made smart choices. Pursued a sensible set of degrees and a career that would support me well into retirement. All the comforts of modern life were at my fingertips. My current dilemma was which Mercedes convertible to buy. Many would say this was a good problem to have – a real first world problem.

But none of that explained the fog and the empty, hollow feeling. And it was growing thicker and stronger by the day.

I took self-help classes at the advice of a friend. Always having been the explorative type, I enjoyed them, but the fog was still there. Maybe I was depressed? I found a great therapist. The fog remained. I could slowly feel my life slipping away, and the scariest part of all was I wasn't sure I really even cared.

One day, stuck in the muck of the fog, I recalled a time in my life when I had taken the Trans-Siberian Railway to China. I had just finished working in London and was about to move to the Netherlands to start my MBA (a very smart and logical next step). I was on the train to Xian, and I met a woman from Australia who was sharing my compartment. She told me she was en-route to a small village in the middle of nowhere to help orphaned children. Instantly I sized her up. Very noble, probably one of those religious zealot do-gooder types, I mused. She had recently sold a very successful chain of daycare centers in Brisbane and now had the financial freedom to do the charity work she enjoyed.

"How nice!" I exclaimed, trying to sound cheerful and supportive.

"It *is* nice," she replied with a warm and contented smile.

Maybe it was her tone of voice that caught me. To this day, I'm not quite sure what it was, but I glanced up from my magazine and then really looked at her this time. And as much as I wanted to write her off as the rah-rah type who drank too much Kool-Aid, I knew I couldn't. She wasn't giving off that vibe.

She had the look of someone who is happy. I mean really happy. Not someone who is faking it or trying too hard, like one of those crazed televangelists. A woman at peace with her life. A woman fulfilled. It was a rare sight, particularly after the dark, cold, and dreary streets of London.

And then I figured, "What the heck. I'll probably never see her again." (And I was right.) For some strange reason I just had to know . . .

"Would you say that you're happy?" I suddenly asked her.

"Yes," she replied immediately without hesitation.

"And why is that?" I wanted to know.

"Because I'm fulfilling my purpose on earth – helping children that need a decent chance in life."

Now I was really curious. This woman had the answer. This woman had managed to find her way out of the fog for good. I could feel it.

"How do you know it's your purpose?" I asked.

"You just know it," she replied with a smile.

Damn! Not what I was expecting. And unfortunately I knew what was coming next.

"What's your purpose?" she asked.

"Well, soon I'll be starting my MBA. I'm not one hundred percent sure what I'll do with it, but I'm really keen to move out of accounting. It's not for me. Maybe something in the line of communications would be a better fit. Or maybe marketing. I'm quite the extrovert. I think it will help with opportunities further down the road. At least that's what everyone says. Seems like the next logical step."

"That's not what I asked," she replied.

Huh?

"What do you mean?" My voice was tense with challenge.

"I didn't ask you what you're doing. I asked you what your purpose in life is. It's a very different question."

Anxiety was brewing by this point. I could feel it rising up in the pit of my stomach. I needed answers to my questions. I wanted to understand how she just "knew" and had figured out all these things. I wanted what she had. I needed what she had. This much I knew.

"I guess I don't really know. I accomplished everything in London that I wanted to do, met all of my financial goals, and am leaving on a high note, which is great."

I paused and thought . . .

"Who am I saying this for? Her or me?"

I knew she didn't care about how much money I had made.

"Cut the crap. Tell her what's really going on . . ."

For some strange reason, I knew it was safe to tell her the truth.

"But I've been feeling this overwhelming sense of frustration . . . maybe restlessness or longing is a better word . . . for quite some time now. Nothing shakes it. I'm hoping this MBA will help. Maybe give me some sort of direction. Energize me hopefully. Give me a new challenge. A fresh start."

There was a long silence before she finally smiled and replied, "Good.

Your spiritual journey has begun."

The train was slowing down.

"Take care, my dear. This is my stop."

And she was gone.

Over the years, I thought about that conversation quite a bit. She could obviously see what I couldn't. She already knew that the MBA, while well intentioned, wouldn't make a hill of beans difference when it came to my underlying feeling of frustration. She could already see I was in the fog, that I was searching for something. She could see so clearly what I couldn't.

I replayed that conversation over and over again with glass after glass of wine and cigarette after cigarette. At this point, the after-work happy hour had become an everyday occurrence. It provided an ever so slight feeling of calm, a moment of fleeting happiness, a slight reprieve each evening from the fog. It faded quickly, and each morning the fog returned. My head was increasingly cloudy from the copious amounts of Chardonnay and Marlboro Lights I was consuming to generate that reprieve.

Drastic times called for drastic measures. One day I woke up and realized that I had two choices – I could carry on as I was and indeed wind up like one of the characters from the bad after-school special Sister Mary had made me watch, or I could do something.

I could make a different choice. I *had* to make a different choice, because the choices I had been so painstakingly hardwired to make up to that point just weren't working, no matter how well-intentioned that hardwiring by others had been. The truth was I was the only one suffering. I mean, as far as I could tell, all those well-intentioned others were off living their lives, probably not worrying too much about little old me.

"I need to go away for a while."

My voice was cracking as I said the words.

"What do you mean?" my boss Timothy asked.

I took a deep breath. This was torture. I wasn't sure I'd be able to choke the words out. I could feel the tears threatening to come.

"Breathe, just breathe, Shelley. You can do this. This isn't a big deal. You've practiced this conversation in your mind so many times. Just say it. Get it out."

"I have to go away for a while, Timothy. I just have to. I'm so sorry, Timothy."

"Now he REALLY looks worried. He's been such a mentor to me. How can I do this to him? How can I scare him like this? Just get your shit together, Shelley. Don't be such a drama queen. Just tell him this was a mistake and leave his office. You're having a bad day. Maybe it's PMS."

I shifted uncomfortably in my chair, but I didn't budge. I knew what I had to do.

"Why?" he asked, his voice full of concern.

"I don't have a choice. I just know."

I paused. My eyes were pleading with him for understanding. "Have you ever had one of those situations in your life when you just knew?"

He looked at me for what felt like forever, then finally, "How long do you think you'll be gone?"

I hesitated, wondering what his reaction would be. I braced myself for the worst.

"Three months, maybe four."

No visible reaction.

"Where will you go? What will you do?"

"To find my mojo. Somehow I've lost it."

I managed a weak smile. (Where had THAT come from? I hadn't practiced that.)

He smiled.

"Come back when you can. We'll be here."

Mind you, he didn't necessarily say that my job would be. But at that moment, I felt a huge sigh of relief. I was free.

Oh crap, now I have to tell my folks.

In September of 2011, I boarded a plane for Los Angeles. I had decided to start my sabbatical with yoga teacher training. A bit of much needed Zen as I began my journey to God knows what.

The night before the course was due to start, I decided to have a last hurrah. I attended a party at a friend's house, drank two bottles of wine, smoked two packs of cigarettes, and passed out at 1 a.m. in front of my TV with a Taco Bell Mexican pizza. I woke up the next morning with the free hot sauce packets they give you in the drive thru stuck to my face. A fitting start for a budding yoga teacher. Namaste.

In my hungover haze, I turned on the TV. *Eat, Pray, Love* had just come out and was playing. I smiled. What a cliché that was the movie that happened to be playing right then. Cliché or not, that was the last cigarette I ever smoked. And now that I think about it, it was also the last Taco Bell Mexican pizza I ever ate.

In the five years since that day, I have quit smoking, lost three dress sizes, stopped propping up the bar at my local pub, completely changed careers, found a fulfilling vocation, started my own business, married Mr. Right, and bought the house of my dreams. (And just in case you're wondering, the MBA did come in handy, especially once I knew what to do with it.)

Now, back to that original question – was it so hard after all? It wasn't difficult at all, once I realized what was missing from my life – namely me.

What I didn't anticipate that morning five years ago was that I was about to begin an incredibly powerful and life-changing journey into mindfulness. The more I learned about mindfulness, the more I integrated it into my daily life. The more I took concrete action (no matter how small that action), the more I transformed.

This book is a summary of what I learned along the way. It's a realistic, practical, and somewhat irreverent view of a topic that, in my humble opinion, is often over-esotericized. (Yes, I made that last word up. It's a pretty good one, don't you think?)

And here's why I say mindfulness has been over-esotericized. (Couldn't resist using it again.) If I had been waiting for that moment of Zen, that feeling of peace we all hear so much about when the discussion turns to mindfulness, I never would have gotten on the plane to go to that yoga teacher training.

In fact, for years I had convinced myself that mindfulness wasn't for me. It was for calm, over-intellectualized, esoteric people. People that like to sit on mats and sip green tea while they listen to chants and the smell of incense wafts around their heads. You know, people who don't have real lives, real cares, real worries.

I was wrong. Dead wrong. Mindfulness is for real people. Tired people. Broken people. Poor people. Angry people. Depressed people. Happy people. Any kind of people.

In other words, it's for the huddled masses.

This book is all about making something seemingly ethereal practical. Actionable. Relatable.

I remember one very valuable story from my yoga teacher training that a senior instructor told us one day. It goes something like this:

An old man who was struggling with his yoga practice walked up to the guru and said, "I just can't do this! I'm not flexible enough. My spine is stiff. My body cannot bend in these ways."

The guru took one long look at him, smiled, and said "Good. Your journey is longer then."

My journey has been long, and it still continues to this day. It continues as I write this book. I don't necessarily have all the answers, but I have asked a lot of questions. And I keep asking them.

Thanks for coming with me on this amazing journey.

Chapter 1

Mindfulness:

It's Not Just for Levitating Monks!

"The fact is, inner peace isn't something that comes when you finally paint the whole house a nice shade of cream and start drinking herbal tea. Inner peace is something that is shaped by the wisdom that 'this too shall pass' and is fired in the kiln of self-knowledge."

~ Tania Ahsan, The Brilliant Book of Calm: Down to Earth Ideas for Finding Inner Peace in a Chaotic World

In this chapter:

- Definition of Mindfulness
- The Human Dog Track
- Activity: Your Most Mindful Moments
- Meet Ed, the Mystical Mindfulness Monk
- Activity: Imagine the Possibilities

A revolution is taking place today. It's subtle, but it's here. And it's growing. You may have heard the word "mindfulness" lately. Maybe it was in *Harvard Business Review*, maybe in *Forbes*. Maybe a colleague mentioned it the other day over lunch. Maybe it was even on *Oprah* of all places. (Yes, I watch her too.) But wherever and however you heard it, mindfulness is here. And it's here for a reason, although perhaps a different one from what some experts will tell you.

Mindfulness is often touted in respected business magazines as a way to increase productivity or a novel way of enhancing your ability to focus. However it's mentioned in these credible sources, it tends to be linked to output. A new way of cramming more tasks into an over-stuffed day – yippee! Now that will make you jump for joy, right? Well, I suppose that's one way of looking at it, although it's a pretty narrow view in my opinion.

So why this mindfulness movement? Does society really need another big buzzword? Or has *Harvard Business Review* run out of topics and is grasping at straws, desperately trying to create another bandwagon to jump on like they did with multi-tasking years ago? Is multi-tasking now out and mindfulness now in? It wouldn't be the first time *HBR* changed tack, and chances are it won't be the last.

Not long ago, I was speaking on the topic of mindfulness at a conference of energy leaders and decided to make the subject as real as I possibly could. After all, time is money, right? Plus I have an as yet under-appreciated knack for breaking down the esoteric into the practical. So I put the subject of mindfulness in the context of an object that just about every person has these days, the smartphone. I thought my choice was particularly relevant considering I had noticed, while sitting in the back of the conference hall, that only 20% of the audience was actually paying attention, while the other 80% displayed the characteristic chin-to-chest smartphone pose we all know so well.

Here's what I told the crowded auditorium. The *Daily Mail* in the UK recently surveyed their readers about how they used their smartphones. This is what they discovered about the average user. He (or she) now:

- Picks up his device more than 1,500 times a week. (That equates to over 200 times a day by the way.)
- First reaches for his phone at 7:31 in the morning.
- Checks personal emails and Facebook before he gets out of bed.
- Uses his phone for three hours and sixteen minutes every day.

And almost four in ten users admit to feeling lost without their devices. Be honest! Don't you feel that pang of loss when you realize you've left your precious smartphone at home? I've heard some folks describe it as feeling naked. (Just admit it – no judgment, I swear!)

To a large extent, you probably already realize you are more than a little attached to your smartphone. If you have kids, you're probably trying to do your best to keep them from turning into little smartphone zombies by wrestling the phone out of their little hands at the dinner table. And to be fair, it's easier to spot these predilections in others. Frankly, I'm just as addicted to my smartphone as the next person, and chances are you are too. The question is *why?*

Think about a dog track. Imagine you're there. The smell of stale beer, the hot dog that's been skewered and rotating in the heater for God only knows how long, the aroma of the man in the seat next to you who's wearing a monster truck and tractor pull shirt . . . But I digress.

Focus on the track itself. You've picked your dog that you're sure is a winner using your tried and true eeny-meeny-miny-moe method. You're excited for the race to begin so you can cash in big. After all, you bet a whole five dollars. This is your moment. You watch the handlers parade the dogs around the track. You watch them load the dogs into their starting cages. 3 . . . . 2 . . . . 1, and they're off! Yippee!!!!!

Focus on the dogs now. They're chasing a small mechanical rabbit around the track. Okay, I realize only a dog would think that weird mechanical thing is a rabbit, but that's the whole point, right? To fool the dogs. And that weird mechanical thing is what fools the dogs and keeps them running.

Now, think about what happens. Do the dogs ever actually get the rabbit, even after they cross the finish line? Well, of course not, you're thinking. That's why they run. And you are right. The dogs run and they run and they run. The next day they wake up and do it all over again. They run and they run and they run. Day after day after day. And they never catch the rabbit.

And that is precisely how most of us live our lives. We run and we run and we run, day after day after day. We chase something that always eludes our grasp. We always want more. We wait for the next big thing, whatever it may be – a new job, a better house, a different spouse. We ache with a yearning that longs to be filled – an ache we feel in the pit of our stomach or a tightness in our chest.

We fill our lives with so many activities and tasks, we're too busy to notice our longing. We find ourselves saying, "When X happens, then I'll be happy." Or, "If only this hadn't happened, then . . ." Or, "Once I've finished Y, then I won't have to worry."

Then, by the time we actually get X or finish Y by hook or by crook, it's too late. The happiness is fleeting because we are now fixated on a new want or we have found a new worry to occupy our time. And so the cycle continues, on and on and on.

And this brings me back to the good old smartphone and the energy leaders' conference. This very important and very expensive conference for which they've paid a fair whack and taken significant time out of busy schedules to attend. And most attendees are spending their time thinking about the next email they need to send, the next thing to cross off their task list, the next phone call they need to make. Well, at least there were free cocktails, and the snacks were good.

In my spare time, when I'm not enjoying free cocktails and tasty snacks at stimulating conferences, I teach yoga. (Yes, I'm one of those people, but I promise I'll keep it real or as real as a yogini ever gets!) I see the yoga equivalent of the dog track and the energy conference all the time. Many of my students literally can't sit still. About 50 minutes into the class, we do a posture called *savasana*. It literally means dead body pose or corpse pose in Sanskrit. I tell my students that it's the easiest posture to learn but the hardest one to actually do.

Savasana is all about slowing down your torrent of thoughts and being in the present moment. For many people, especially beginners, this is just too much. I see students fidgeting, blowing their noses, picking lint off their yoga leotard, playing with their water bottles, deciding that this exact moment of *savasana* is when they absolutely have to leave the room to use the bathroom. It's quite impressive the things we do to distract ourselves. And that's why *savasana* is often considered the most difficult posture there is in yoga.

So why do we humans torture ourselves in this way? And that is an excellent question! And a lot of famous philosophers, spiritual gurus, and other assorted personal development experts have built careers and made a lot of money trying to figure this one out.

Is it that humans have an innate aversion to being bored? Maybe. Or perhaps it's the constant messages we're bombarded with these days that exhort us to live big. Aren't these messages really telling us that we're not enough? And doesn't that set us up to be continually worried about achieving more so we can finally be enough? Maybe. Or perhaps, if we slow down, we're afraid to sit with ourselves and face who we really are. Maybe that's what scares the bejeezus out of us. Maybe.

The bottom line is no one really knows why we live on autopilot 99% of the time. I will even dare to suggest the answer is slightly different for each person. I'm also going to dare to suggest you start to look deep within yourself so you can begin to unravel the mystery behind your eternal human rabbit-chasing restlessness.

What's all this got to do with mindfulness? Everything. Mindfulness is the practice that, over time, shines light on this dark, unconscious cycle. And let's be clear. Mindfulness is *not* about reducing drive or ambition. Drive and ambition are important. The interesting thing about mindfulness is that, when practiced consistently, it often aids in the achievement of goals.

On that point, I've prepared the following handy dandy chart for you, as there are many common misconceptions about what mindfulness is and isn't. Over the course of this book, all of the below will be explained, and many great mindfulness mysteries will be revealed.

Mindfulness IS	Mindfulness ISN'T
• Being present and focused	• Zoning out in some sort of strange trance
• Listening intently	• Losing ambition
• Awareness of your thoughts and feelings	• Having to be happy and "zenned out" all the time
• Choosing your reaction to a situation	• Getting less done
• Neutrality and non-judgment	• Joining some hippie commune out west (not unless you really want to of course
• Genuine curiosity	– no judgment!)

Mindfulness is about putting your attention where it really matters – on the present moment. Not on the past as we often like to do. And not on the future like the dogs at the track constantly chasing a rabbit they'll never catch or the distracted conference goers thinking about the next email. Mindfulness is about the present which, I would argue, is the only thing we ever really have. Nothing ever happens in the past or in the future. It happens now. Just think about that for a second. I mean really think. When did anything in your life ever happen in the past or in the future? The answer is never. Your life happens in the present. It happens now.

Definition of Mindfulness: The practice of focusing awareness on the present moment non-judgmentally.

Simple, right? But, like most simple concepts, it isn't necessarily easy. I also like to define it as being "in the zone" or "in the flow." I'll give you an example of one of my most mindful moments that really stands out for me.

I was working on my MBA at the Rotterdam School of Management in the Netherlands. I had recently entered my second year of the program, and I recall the incoming batch of first-year MBA students being a particularly whiny and difficult bunch. Among their many complaints was the fact that the accounting professor was sub-par, and therefore they weren't learning enough.

Why anyone would really want to learn a lot about accounting was beyond me! I already had a master's in the subject, and the first few years of practice had driven me straight to the bottle because I found it so tedious and boring. (My apologies to any of my accountant readers who do not find it boring and who do not drink too much.) However, in a fit of altruism uncharacteristic of me in those days, I publicly committed to save the day and announced I would create and deliver a lecture on financial accounting open to anyone who wanted to attend.

The day was swiftly approaching. Like the good ostrich that I am, I had stuck my head in the sand and had tried to forget about the session, secretly hoping no one would bother to show up. I was heading home on the train from Amsterdam after a night of partying and revelry, when I decided it would probably be good idea to have a plan for the next day. I went the extra mile in my hungover haze and even prepared PowerPoint slides, complete with sample accounting problems for the eager first-years to work – a particularly generous gesture I thought.

I arrived at the lecture hall the next day and was shocked to discover sixty first-years waiting for me. It was a full house, standing room only. And, before I even had a chance to get nervous, it was show time! So I started to teach. And it was magic. I looked down at my watch at the end of the session, and two and a half hours had passed. It had felt more like five minutes. How could this be?

Like I said before, accounting for me is right up there with watching paint dry. Or maybe it's more like getting a tooth pulled – a necessary evil. So it wasn't the accounting that made me lose track of time. That's when I realized I love to teach. What was even more amazing was that I was good at it! To prove it, my students gave me a standing ovation at the end of the session. You have to admit that's no small feat considering we're talking about accounting, right? (Again, apologies to my accountant readers.)

Activity: Your Most Mindful Moments

Let's try an exercise. I want you to think about moments when you've been in the zone, in the flow. When did time stop and you become totally absorbed in what was going on? I'm serious about this exercise. Find a comfortable spot to sit. Do it now. Close your eyes. Now spend five minutes thinking about those moments in your life when you were totally present, totally mindful. Imagine yourself reliving them. Done? Okay. Now, write down what you saw and felt. When you've finished writing, answer the following questions.

1. Where were you?

_____

_____

_____

_____

_____

2. What were you doing?

_____

_____

_____

_____

_____

3. Who were you with?

_____

_____

_____

_____

_____

4. How did you feel? What words would you use to describe this feeling?

_____

_____

_____

_____

_____

Quite often I hear things like:

Celebrating something important with friends and family

Walking in the woods

Playing with my dog

Holding my children

Eating an amazing piece of cheesecake (my personal favorite)

Watching a beautiful sunset

Helping someone less fortunate

Working in my garden

Cooking a meal

Words that I hear to describe feelings are:

Connected

Passionate

Purposeful

Alive

Happy

Excited

Joyful

Electric

Ecstatic

And this is what it means to live mindfully.

Now at this point you may be saying to yourself,

> *"Many of the things listed above are pretty ordinary, e.g. cooking a meal. I cook all the time, and I don't feel elated when I do it. I feel put out and resentful. This is B.S. How can this be? You're mindful when you meditate maybe. Or maybe if you have a once in a lifetime kind of experience, like the birth of a child. Not everything can be done mindfully."*

But that's not true. You have just made my point for me. Thank you. That's exactly the point. ANYTHING and I repeat ANYTHING can be mindful. It's not the WHAT you do, but the HOW you do it. Let's repeat that. It's not the WHAT you do, but the HOW you do it.

In other words, it's not what you're doing but how you're actually doing it that makes it either mindful or mindless. Let me give you a very simple example – brushing your teeth. There are two ways of looking at brushing your teeth. The first, which is pretty uninspiring, is that it's a tedious chore you need to get through as quickly as possible so you can move on to the next latest and greatest thing on your list like taking out the trash. This is how most of us view brushing our teeth.

Your second option is to approach brushing your teeth as an experience. The experience of actually tasting the toothpaste, feeling the brush against your teeth, feeling how clean your teeth are right after you've brushed. Go ahead. Try it the next time you brush your teeth. I dare you! Focus on just the act of brushing itself and nothing else. Don't think about that next email you need to send or that next chore you need to do until after you've finished brushing. You'll notice a difference, I promise.

The reality is you have opportunities all around you all the time to practice mindfulness every day, whether you're mindful of it or not. (Ha! I just told a little mindfulness joke. Okay, so it was a teeny tiny mindfulness joke. Geesh. Everyone's a critic.)

And this leads to my next point about what a mindful person really looks like – fact versus fiction. When I speak on this topic, it's not uncommon for folks to conjure up images of a wise sage of a monk, floating on a cloud of air, hair flowing in the breeze along with his beautiful robe. Say hello to Ed.

Ed, The Mystical Mindfulness Monk, who moonlights in his spare time as the unachievable standard we all hold ourselves to where this particular subject is concerned. Or, put another way, Ed is the excuse why we don't try mindfulness in the first place. C'mon. You can't tell me you haven't thought at least once to yourself that mindfulness is for "those people." You know, the yoga-practicing, vegan-eating, tree-hugging, flowy clothes-wearing, incense-burning, crystal-hoarding folks like Ed here.

Well, I'm here to burst your bubble. Mindfulness isn't just something the Eds of the world can do. Mindfulness is something anyone can do. Including you.

Activity: Imagine the Possibilities

Think back to your mindful moments that you listed in the previous exercise.

1. If you could increase these moments by 50%, what would the impact be on your life?

_____

_____

_____

_____

_____

2. What about 100%?

_____

_____

_____

_____

_____

3. Or even 1000%?

_____

_____

_____

_____

_____

Powerful, isn't it? The more you practice mindfulness, the more of these moments you will have. I'm living proof.

In summary:

- Mindfulness is the practice of focusing awareness on the present moment non-judgmentally. Or, in other words, it's those moments when you feel in the zone, in the flow, when time appears to stop or stand still.

- Mindfulness is about listening with intention, curiosity, non-judgment, and awareness of your thoughts and emotions. It's not about losing ambition, having to be happy and "zenned out" all the time, or getting less done.

- Mindfulness is for anyone, anywhere – not just the Mystical Mindfulness Monks of the world.

- It's not the what, but the how. In other words, it's not what you do but how you do it that makes it mindful or mindless. Even brushing your teeth can be a mindfulness practice.

In the next chapter, we'll be exploring that most famous of Stephen Covey quotes, "Begin with the end in mind," as we delve into life intentions. And why all the fuss over just one sentence? As you will soon see, it's one little sentence that makes a heck of a difference.

Chapter 2

Creating a Life Intention:

One Little Sentence That Makes a Big Difference

"If you don't know where you're going, any road will take you there."

~ *The Cheshire Cat, Alice in Wonderland Through the Looking Glass*

In this chapter:

- The $64,000 Question

- My Medusa

- Definition of a Life Intention

- Activity: That's What I Want!

- Activity: Visualization

- The Hero's Journey

- Activity: Connecting Your Dots

- Activity: Your Life Intention Statement

I have often thought about the Cheshire Cat. Particularly, that he really knew a thing or two about life, especially when it comes to mindfulness. When I think about the above quote, I'm reminded of a TV commercial I saw once for monster.com. It featured young children saying things like "When

I grow up I want to file all day. Claw my way up to middle management. Be replaced on a whim. Be a yes man. A yes woman. Underappreciated . . ."

At the end of the ad, a question pops up on the screen, "What did you want to be?" It's a great question. It's the $64,000 question that is often scary because it may expose just how far we have allowed ourselves to drift through life rather aimlessly and haphazardly. Our train has gotten off track, if it was ever on it to begin with.

The other day, I was teaching a mindfulness course, and one of my students exclaimed, "Have you ever just stopped and thought how the hell did I end up here? I mean, really? Doing what I'm doing. Working where I'm working. This isn't what I intended for my life. I'm not sure what I was intending, but I can tell you this isn't it."

Just about every head in the room was nodding vigorously, mine included. It brings back memories of that time not long ago when my life felt hopelessly stuck. I was slugging away each day, and while everything looked great on paper, I was too embarrassed to admit I was miserable and unfulfilled. I remember thinking over and over again:

"Is this it? There has to be more to life than this. What's wrong with me? Everyone else seems to be happy (or at least that's what their Facebook statuses were indicating). What am I not getting?"

So I decided to ask myself the exact question my student posed as it related to that point in my life and, in doing so, I remembered something.

A seemingly insignificant event that set me on the long and rather meandering path to nonfulfillment.

I was four years old and attending the pre-school down the street from our house. It was art time. And there we were, ten little girls, each seated in front of a cold, gray lump of clay. I looked at my lump for a while, and then inspiration struck. Seized by my idea, I meticulously worked, fashioning my cold gray lump into a work of art. I was focused. In the zone. Deep in the throes of mindfulness, although my four-year-old brain knew nothing of this.

Finally, I stopped sculpting and looked at what I had created. There she was in all her glory. A statue of Medusa. Complete with long flowing hair made of snakes. She was beautiful. She was glorious.

"Who's that?" asked my teacher.

"Medusa, the Greek goddess with snakes for hair," I calmly replied, thinking it should have been obvious, you stupid woman.

"How amazing!" exclaimed my teacher. "Look, girls, at this amazing figurine! Isn't it creative?"

I was glowing. And frankly I should have been. What four-year-old knows who Medusa is? And not only did I know, I had managed to fashion her out of clay, to boot.

Beaming from ear to ear, I turned towards the other girls to look at what they had made, and my smile quickly faded. Staring back at me were nine lopsided pots. I started to blush. Fear and anxiety set in, and I got that sinking feeling in my stomach. You know the one. I knew what I had to do in that moment. I looked down at Medusa, lifted my little hand, and with great sadness smashed her in one fell swoop. And then I made a pot.

It was at that exact moment, unconscious as it was, I decided that creativity was something I could live without. Something I didn't need. And who can blame me? What little four-year-old girl doesn't want to belong?

What I didn't know at the time is that just one choice can have far-reaching consequences. That very innocent, unconscious, seemingly insignificant choice would come back to bite me in the butt. Over and over and over again.

Fast forward twenty years, and you'll find me staring at an Excel spreadsheet, bored out of my mind, for ten plus hours a day. Then trudging either home to do it all over again the next day or to the pub to find some much needed liquid inspiration.

If only I hadn't smashed that damn statue.

Now, this isn't to say that I would have ended up the next Frida Kahlo if I had kept the Medusa. I'm sure my current art teacher will attest to that. However, I never gave myself the chance to find out. Instead, I buried this aspect of my personality and blindly proceeded to follow a very stable, sensible and respectable career path that made a great deal of logical sense but didn't connect with my heart – accounting. And let me tell you, it was a painful case of square peg, round hole from day one.

The bottom line (I still speak Accountant Speak) is that we all have a Medusa or two in our past. A part of ourselves that we've never really expressed. Perhaps something that we've disallowed because it was different, silly, or how the heck are we ever going to make money with that. And slowly, over time, we lose touch with these parts of ourselves. We drift along unconsciously, busy chasing that mechanical rabbit, caught up in the game of life. And then we wake up one day and wonder, just like my student, "How the hell did I get here?"

But instead of doing something about it, we keep plodding along, usually thinking that we're the only one who feels this way. That maybe, if we just keep plodding along, things will eventually change. (Chances are they won't – just in case you were wondering.) Or we silently curse ourselves for feeling this way and wonder why everyone else seems so happy. So together. (Chances are they're not – just in case you were wondering.)

This is why life intention statements are so important. And why the topic is numero uno on my agenda for the mindfulness course that I teach. It's also an exercise that can be uncomfortable for students for a number of reasons. Perhaps we've shut down so many parts of ourselves that we're totally confused and have no idea what we really want. Or else we're too busy being superman or superwoman to our loved ones to think about what we may want and need. After all, only selfish people think about things like life intentions. Or heck! Who has time for this malarkey? There's work to be done! Or you can insert your own excuse. This is just a handful of what I've seen and heard (and said).

And just what is a life intention statement you ask? Excellent question. When I ask folks the meaning of the word intention, I often hear the word goal. And that is indeed true. And we may have many, many goals in life, such as:

- Make a million dollars, be financially stable, or whatever floats your financial boat
- Get that prized promotion at work so that at long last it'll be your

name on that door, and you'll finally get the good parking spot

- Raise high-functioning kids that don't live at home at age thirty and keep asking for beer money
- Travel the world, see exciting places, meet new people, enjoy interesting food (hopefully without getting sick from the oh so tasty street snacks)
- Get really fit and win the Tour De France (hopefully without the performance enhancing drugs because no one likes a cheater)

The difference between these types of goals, which are very important by the way, and a life intention statement is that the latter sums up the very purpose and essence of your life. It's the reason you were put on this earth. And while a million dollars is very nice to have, I'm here to tell you it's not the reason you were put on this earth. Now, what you do with it, on the other hand, may be.

A life intention statement is the one sentence that keeps you grounded. It's that one sentence you remember when faced with setbacks that keeps you going no matter how bad your day is. It's that one sentence that keeps you on track, even when you're busy chasing that mechanical rabbit, as we all do.

All this to say that a mindful life is an intentional life. It's a conscious life. I have often mused that writing a life intention statement is the greatest act of self-love a person can show themselves. Or, if self-love doesn't float your boat, it's also the greatest way to hone your focus and get sh#t done. The bottom line is, (there's that Accountant Speak again) the more conscious a person is about what they want, the greater their chances of achieving it. So, with all that said, over the next few exercises, you're going to build your own personal life intention statement. We'll be taking this baby step by baby step to really get the creative juices flowing.

Not-so-subtle Advice Disclaimer: If I were sitting right next to you right now, I would grab your arm and say, "Stop! Put the book down! Right now! Okay. Now look into my eyes. This is the most important thing in this whole book. Don't just keep reading. Do the exercises. Now!" But since I'm not sitting right next to you (my loss), all I can do is implore you to take the time and do this activity. Don't skip over it, telling yourself you'll come back to it after you've read the book. We both know you won't.

Just saying. You may proceed now.

Activity: That's What I Want! (Cue the inspirational music here)

Step 1: Grab a sheet of paper and draw a large circle in the center. Perfectionist disclaimer: If it's lopsided, no worries. I'll let you off the hook.

Step 2: Inside the circle, write down words that express everything you want from life. Some examples might be:

- Things, e.g. a house in that location you've always wanted
- Experiences you'd like to have, e.g. write a cool book on mindfulness

- States of being/emotions, e.g. love
- People, e.g. a caring partner

Give yourself a good 10 minutes, and write down everything that comes to mind. And here's the most important detail – don't filter it! Allow yourself to be free from constraints. Don't get caught up in what's most feasible or realistic, like we silly adults often do. For the purposes of this exercise, anything is possible.

Let your thoughts flow onto the paper one by one without editing yourself.

Step 3: Now, outside the circle, I want you to write down everything you don't want from life. Again, these could be things, experiences, states of being, emotions, people.

Give yourself another full 10 minutes for this step, and write down everything that comes to mind.

Step 4: When you're finished with step 3, spend a few minutes taking a look at everything you've written down, particularly the things you want. Write down anything you notice about the two lists.

So why did I have you do this? A perfectly reasonable question, and the answer is actually quite simple. Think back to my distressed student for a minute. "This isn't what I intended for my life. I'm not sure what I was intending, but I can tell you this isn't it."

The interesting thing about life is that many of us go through it focusing on what we don't want. I don't want any more money problems. I don't want to stay in this dead-end job. I don't want to have to see my mother-in-law. I don't want to feel unfulfilled. I don't want to be afraid. I don't want this season of *Breaking Bad* to end. Whatever.

There are several biological reasons why our mind tends to gravitate towards the negative that have to do with the fight or flight reflex and the fact that our mind is constantly scanning our external environment for threats. But let's keep things simple, shall we?

Let's say you look down at your hand tomorrow, and you notice a small bump.

Day 1: Hmmm, I wonder what that is.

Day 2: Hmmm, has it gotten bigger from yesterday? I think it's gotten bigger from yesterday. I wonder if I should Google this.

Day 3: Oh wow, Google says it could be a cyst. Or maybe it's a wart. Yuck. That's disgusting. Oh God, what if it is? What do I do about it? Maybe if I just poke at it a bit, it will go away.

Day 4: Oh God, it definitely is bigger now! I guess I shouldn't have poked at it. Maybe I should go down to the pharmacy and get some of that wart removal cream. Yeah, that will do the trick. Okay, "Apply cream and put Band-Aid on top. Do not remove Band-Aid."

Day 5: I wonder if it's working. I need to check to make sure it's working. I'll just take the Band-Aid off now and have a little peek. Oh my God, it's not working! Now it looks like I have a rash. I wonder if I'm allergic to this cream. Maybe I need to go to the doctor? Ugggh . . . I really don't have time to go to the doctor this week.

And after an expensive and time-consuming doctor's visit that you really didn't have time for, you realize that everything would have been okay if only you had just taken your own advice in the first place and left it alone.

All this to say, what we focus on persists. What we focus on typically intensifies. And whether we realize it or not, we have a choice which side of the circle we focus on.

Okay, now that you've got a clearer sense of the things you want in your life, let's take this one step further. What would it actually look like if you were living inside the circle on a daily basis? In order to delve into your inner circle further and get really crystal clear, we're going to use a very powerful tool called visualization.

Activity: Visualization

Find a comfortable spot. Set a timer for ten or fifteen minutes. Read the following through first, then close your eyes and actually do it. (Unless you can read with your eyes closed, which would be a really cool trick.) And if you can't be bothered to try it that way, you can also download an audio from my website of me reading the visualization to you. (I've been told I have a really lovely voice – just in case you're interested.) www. truenorthlifecoach.com/resources

Visualization

Imagine yourself in a peaceful meadow. You're walking through the tall grass that's blowing in the wind. You hear the sound of the grass rustling in the wind. The sun is shining. You look up and see beautiful birds high in the sky.

You keep walking, all the time you're smiling, taking in this peaceful experience.

You see a rock in front of you. You stop at the rock and look to the right. When you look to the right, you see a vision. The vision you see is yourself, living your ideal life. Where are you? What are you doing? Who are you with? What possessions do you have? How do you feel?

You stop and spend a few moments taking it all in. The people you're with, the places you're at, the possessions you have, the things you're doing, the way you're feeling.

As you watch this vision, you are filled with a sense of opportunity and possibility.

You now know that it's time to leave the rock and this vision. You turn around and start walking back in the direction that you came.

Open your eyes now.

Perfectionist Disclaimer: It's okay if you don't imagine it exactly as I have written it. I will forgive you. There is no perfect field, no perfect bird, no perfect rock. Just get on with it!

Now, answer the following questions:

1. Where were you?

_____

_____

_____

_____

2. What were you doing?

_____

_____

_____

_____

3. Who were you with?

_____

_____

_____

_____

_____

4. What possessions did you have?

_____

_____

_____

_____

_____

5. How did you feel?

_____

_____

_____

_____

_____

Now you may have noticed some differences between your current reality and this vision. If you find yourself going to the dark side, you may even start to think things like, "How has my life gotten so massively off track?" Or "Nice dream, but that's never going to happen."

Then cue the resentment, anger, frustration, sadness, embarrassment, disappointment, despair, or whatever negative emotion you try to avoid that you tend to use to beat yourself up at these introspective points. No sweat. It's all perfectly natural. And can be very helpful if we know what to do with it.

Think about it. If we were comfortable where we were, we would stay there forever. I've always thought that, ultimately, human beings are like water. We always take the path of least resistance – which works just fine and dandy right up until the point when the dam breaks.

We all do our best to try to avoid pain, but often it's simply an indicator that something needs to change in order for us to grow. And this is such a universal truth that a guy by the name of Joseph Campbell spent his entire career proving it by studying in mind-numbing detail every great mythology since the dawn of time. He even coined a little phrase called the Hero's Journey. If you haven't heard of it, you're definitely familiar with it. It's pretty much the plot for any epic tale that's ever been told, and it goes something like this:

1. Man (or Woman, let's be fair here) encounters a challenge/new adventure.

2. Man gallops off on his Trusty White Horse to take on said challenge (onward ho!) and falls flat on his face.

3. Man experiences pain and confusion, wanders in the wilderness licking his wounds and feeling sorry for himself, and finally pulls his head out of his rear end, which results in personal growth and new insight.

4. Using new insight, Man valiantly slays the Dragon, woos his Lady Love, and returns to his Chosen People, ready to lead them into a bright new era.

5. The End.

Sound familiar? Think *Star Wars*, think *Top Gun*, think *Out of Africa* even (my favorite movie, in case you were wondering). If you look hard enough, you'll find this theme in just about every story you read in a book or watch on a screen.

Okay, so what's the point of this fun little diversion? The point is we all have times in life when we feel we're hugely off track. We feel the pain and confusion, just like our little hero on his trusty horse. We wander in the wilderness of our life, lacking direction, running from one task to the next, wondering if this is all there is.

And that is where true transformation lies. It often reminds me of that line from a Leonard Cohen song, "There's a crack in everything. That's how the light gets in." Quite poetic in my not so humble opinion. The trick is to keep perspective and keep connecting the dots in your story, because ultimately you are the one that gets to write the ending. Heck, when you get right down to it, you're writing the whole darned story one way or the other. You're either writing it intentionally or you're not. Your choice.

Connecting the dots? What do I mean by this? Okay, here's an example:

Dot #1:   If I hadn't majored in accounting and spent all that time whittling away at Excel spreadsheets, I never would have had the opportunity to go to London.

Dot #2: If I hadn't gone to London, I never would have gotten burnt out, emotionally cracked myself up, spent copious hours in the pub, and wanted to jump off a twelve-story building.

Dot #3: And if all that hadn't happened, I never would have discovered the wonderful world of yoga and mindfulness.

Dot #4: If I hadn't discovered yoga and mindfulness, I never would have figured out how to change my career and would have been stuck counting beans till the cows came home. Moo.

Dot #5: If I hadn't changed careers, I never would have been able to move to a cool place full of hipsters and over-priced lattes like Austin, Texas and hang out and write books like the one you're reading now.

Take a moment and try it for yourself.

Activity: Connecting Your Dots

1. Where in your life do you feel stuck right now?

_____

_____

_____

_____

_____

2. How could this experience be preparing you for something bigger down the road?

_____

_____

_____

_____

_____

All right, now it's time for the final step – writing that life intention statement. You know what you want and you have a sense of what your ideal life looks like. Now it's time to generate that one sentence that will help you stay on track. Your own personal mantra. And just think, you didn't have to trek up the Himalayas to find Ed, The Mystical Mindfulness Monk for it!

Activity: Your Life Intention Statement

Spend 10-15 minutes answering the following questions:

1. Think about your unique gifts. The one thing that makes me really unique is:

_____

_____

_____

_____

_____

2. Think about what you would like to see happen globally, locally, or in any aspect of your life. The one thing I'd like to experience most in my lifetime is:

_____

_____

_____

_____

_____

3. Think about, at your core, what you really want out of life personally and emotionally. The one thing I want most out of life is:

_____

_____

_____

_____

_____

Now, all you need to do is fill in the blanks.

My life intention is to use my **(your unique gift from #1)** to accomplish **(one thing you'd like to experience from #2)** and in so doing achieve **(one thing you want most out of life from #3)**.

Voila! You've just written your own personalized life intention statement. You now have your mantra that would even make the likes of Ed jealous.

Perfectionist Disclaimer: This life intention statement is a living, breathing statement. You can revisit it as much as you like. It can often change with time. You don't just get one shot at this and then that's it. The goal is not to write the "right" intention statement. It doesn't have to be high and mighty. It doesn't have to be about saving the children or creating world peace. You don't need to bounce this off 10 people, take a poll, conduct a focus group, or ask for permission. The goal is to write the statement that resonates most with you. When you have it right, you'll feel it in your gut. Your intuition will kick in. You'll just KNOW.

And if you're having problems with knowing what KNOWING feels like, keep reading. Mindfulness practices are great for cultivating intuition. Meditation, which I'll be talking about in a later chapter, is one of the best practices there is for honing your keen (or not so keen) sense of intuition.

Now, my advice is to put this statement up somewhere visible. Maybe in your office, maybe on your bathroom mirror. Any place where you will be sure to see it regularly. Memorize it. Keep it in the front of your mind as much as possible. And if you do, you'll start to notice a few things.

First, you'll be clearer on your priorities and what's important to you. Second, the sense of purpose this statement generates will make you feel lighter and more energized. And finally, my personal favorite, you'll find it easier to say no (politely) to things you really don't want to do. I don't know about you, but that seems like a heck of a lot of benefit for writing one little itty bitty life intention statement.

In summary:

- A strong life intention is the key to living mindfully. After all, if you don't know where you're going, any road will take you there.

- In life, we often focus on what we don't want. The result is just typically more of what we don't want. A more helpful perspective is to focus on what you do want.

- We all get off track from time to time. Remember the Hero's Journey and think about what you can learn from the experience. When you're stuck, connect the dots. How might this experience be preparing you for something bigger?

- Your life intention statement is the mantra for your life that will help keep you on track. There is no right or wrong. It isn't meant to be perfect. It's meant to resonate with you at an intuitive level.

- Your life intention is a living, breathing statement. It may change over time as you grow and encounter new experiences and challenges. It adapts as you do.

So now that you've got your handy dandy life intention statement and you feel like you've finally gotten your train back on track, don't get too comfortable yet. We're going to spend the next chapter looking at a little thing called judgment, and I'm including some special tools for reining it in because, more often than not, it will rear its ugly little head and send your mindfulness choo-choo careening right off the track.

Chapter 3

Judgment:

Why You're Better Off Leaving It to Judge Judy

"I never approve, or disapprove, of anything now.

It is an absurd attitude to take towards life."

~ *Oscar Wilde, The Picture of Dorian Gray*

In this chapter:

- The Definition of Mindfulness (again)

- Activity: Your Lisa

- Judgment vs. Discernment

- Activity: Reframing Limiting Beliefs

- Impostor Syndrome

- Self-Compassion: The Antidote to Judgment

- Activity: What Labels Do I Choose?

In August of 2015, a month after I packed in my job and started my own company, I decided to reward myself with a two-week meditation retreat. A few weeks of blissful self-reflection in the wilds of the Colorado mountains, I mused. A fitting start for a trail-blazing woman who has just left the madness of the corporate grind to embark on a new journey and start a business focused on personal development. It reminds me of that saying, "The road to hell is paved with good intentions." Perhaps you've heard of it?

The setting was indeed idyllic. I spent the two weeks in a tent in a very remote part of the Colorado mountains with 120 other brave souls. So idyllic, in fact, that often a chipmunk or deer would wander in during meditation sessions and stare at the strange humans sitting on mats, staring off into space for hours on end. I often spent hours longing to be one of those deer. At least I could have escaped.

The night before the retreat started, we gathered together for an orientation. During that session, it became clear to me that the meditation retreat really was just that – meditating. All day long. No rest for the weary. Sitting was to start at 7 am and end each evening around 9 pm.

And it was at that exact moment that the panic started to set in. Two weeks? Two weeks of sitting on a mat? My legs will go numb. My back will give out. I'll die of boredom. And it was just at that precise moment, in my infinite wisdom, I realized I had inadvertently signed up for two weeks of my worst fear. For some people it's snakes. For some it's death. I, however, fear boredom and will do just about anything to avoid it.

I have often thought to myself, "How could I have been so stupid?" (Which would be judgment, by the way, but we'll get into that later.) And it's true. It was indeed billed as a meditation retreat – make no mistake. But often the mind sees and interprets what it wants to see and interpret.

When I came across the event for the first time on the internet, my mind conjured up images not only of me sitting peacefully in the woods with the deer and chipmunk in blissful harmony, but also hours of me sitting with fellow meditators, discussing the mysteries of life. Musing about the great Buddhist concepts of dharma and perhaps even samsara. Two weeks full of stimulating intellectual conversation that would feed my mind and spirit. Nope and nope. It was basically two weeks of sitting on a bumpy mat.

After the first day, I was convinced I was going to claw my eyes out. Between sitting sessions, I sought out other like-minded meditators for much needed conversation where I blurted out an endless stream of fears and concerns.

To make matters worse, every few days, the meditation instructors upped the ante and added some new torture. A week in, they had us practicing mindful eating in the Zen Buddhist style of oryoki. A bizarre ritual for one unaccustomed to the practice. By the time all 120 participants had been served, and a barrage of chants had been chanted and rituals completed, the food was cold. After eating my meal in silence, I was responsible for cleaning my bowls myself with tepid water and reassembling the oryoki set (which was always a bit of a mystery to me considering

I hadn't really been paying attention the day they explained how to do it . . . oops). I found myself regressing to my childhood days and became one of the troublemakers of my eating group. The art of making faces while trying to eat an avocado and sour cream with chopsticks became my new skill. Ed would have been less than impressed.

And then the unthinkable happened. The lead meditation instructor announced that the retreat was to become completely silent. No talking, even between the sitting sessions during breaks. Not one single word. If there was an emergency, we were to write a note.

Now, if you're an introvert, you're probably thinking no biggie. My husband is one and would be perfectly content to live out in a shack all by himself with no other human contact for weeks on end. I don't get it, but different strokes for different folks I've always said. If you happen to be the other half of the population that's an extrovert, you will quickly understand my plight.

Resigned to my new silent fate, the next morning I was sitting on my mat, under the guise of meditation:

"Uuuugh, I hope Eric doesn't sit next to me again. He smells. It's so disgusting, I don't think he's taken a bath since he's been here. Why do I always get stuck next to the smelly person? Doesn't he have any respect for his fellow meditators?

There's Janice, she's looking at me again. I can't stand her. So high and mighty. Thinks that, just because she's writing a book, she's so much better than us. So condescending. She was bossy the other day when we were working meal service together. No wonder she's single. No self-respecting guy would put up with that. She must be really insecure. It's always the really bossy types that are super insecure on the inside.

And here comes Dawn. What a weirdo. And dreads are always so stupid on white people. We don't have the right type of hair to wear them. Plus they just end up smelling. She probably lives out in California like all the other beatniks out there that are trying to sell you over-priced ayurvedics. What a scam."

And hence we finally arrive back at the topic of this chapter. Judgment. It was at that precise moment on that bumpy mat that it finally dawned on me. I was a judgment-making machine. My mind was a runaway freight train high on judgment. When you're silent, you have no choice but to notice your judgment. Those sneaky meditation instructors whom I had previously dismissed as hippie-dippies (could that be judgment too?) were really on to something.

So what does judgment have to do with mindfulness? It's a question I've asked myself many a time. And in order to answer it properly, let's go back to the definition of mindfulness, shall we?

Definition of Mindfulness: The practice of focusing awareness on the present moment non-judgmentally.

Okay, so judgment (or rather non-judgment) is in the definition. That much is clear. But why? Isn't mindfulness all about just being in the present moment? Being in the zone? And indeed this is true. So think back to those moments when you're really mindful, per the Your Most Mindful Moments exercise in Chapter 1. Maybe for you it's taking your dog for a quiet walk in the woods. Now, how often during that mindful walk did you find yourself saying this kind of thing to yourself? "This sunset really isn't all that great. I wish I had a better dog. Those flowers really aren't that colorful."

If you were really being mindful, chances are you weren't thinking these things. You were, you know, just enjoying the walk. Just being there in the moment with Fluffy. **When you're fully present and fully aware, you're busy experiencing life, rather than judging or labeling it**. You are busy just being.

When I lecture on mindfulness, I often ask the question, "What does removing judgment allow for?" The answer I'm looking for is only one word. (Remember, I like to keep things simple.)

Possibility.

When you're deep in judgment, whether it's so-called positive or negative judgment, everything appears slightly distorted. It's the equivalent of wearing glasses that are slightly out of focus. What you see is very real to you, but if you were to put on a pair of new lenses, your vision would change. Which one is true? Which one is right? The answer is both. Both are equally valid and true when you're wearing the lenses.

Let me give you an example of what I mean. It would probably be fair to characterize my relationship with my sister Lisa as a challenging one, if you were to look at our past history. We were often at odds, my sister being the practical jokester of the two of us. I recall a phase she went through when she thought it would be really fun to scare me and bought a collection of very realistic plastic roaches from the joke shop. I retaliated by sitting on her. I was the older sister, albeit only by two years, but I was twice her size. My taste for Little Debbie snack cakes gave me a distinct advantage where inflicting pain was concerned.

Over the years, my view of my sister transitioned from one of her being merely troublesome to one of her being Miss Bossy Boots. Always trying to tell me what to do. Always trying to meddle in my life.

I had concocted a number of theories that explained Lisa's bossy behavior. I spent many hours pondering these theories, thinking of examples from our childhood to support my hypothesis. One of my favorite theories was that, because she was the younger sister, she was often living in my older and wiser shadow. This dynamic had given her an inferiority complex where she always had to be right.

Things came to a head when my husband and I got engaged. We were thinking of possibilities for the wedding, and the idea of traveling to Hawaii came up in passing. The next day I received an email from Lisa that was full of links to Hawaiian ideas for weddings.

"How dare she?! She's already trying to tell me how to have

my wedding! I can't believe this. She's always trying to tell me what to do! It never stops. Why can't she just mind her own business and butt out!"

I was relating these frustrations to my soon-to-be husband who patiently and silently waited until I finished my tirade.

"You know what's interesting?"

"What?!" I replied.

"That with the exact same evidence, I would have drawn a completely different conclusion. Perhaps she's just trying to be helpful."

Damn engineer. So logical. I have to admit his statement caught me completely by surprise. Helpful? Not typically a word I would have ever used in relation to my sister.

I decided to sit and ponder this concept for a while and when I did, I realized something. The more labels I used, the more I narrowed Lisa's and my relationship. The more names I called her, the less scope there was for any kind of relationship beyond an adversarial one.

So which one was true? Was she bossy or helpful? At that point, I realized that it didn't really matter. I asked myself a different question. Which story served me best? It's a question I often use these days when I find myself caught up in one of my stories. It's a question I often ask my coaching clients.

I use the term "story" for a reason. We judge people; we judge situations.

Then our minds get to work coming up with intricate stories that justify the judgment we have rendered. We pick up the phone and call girlfriends, boyfriends, family members – anyone who will listen to our stories and tell us we are right. Because that's what judgment is ultimately about. It's about who is right and who is wrong.

Then the next time we see this particular person or find ourselves in that specific situation, the back story is running the entire time. Which makes it impossible to be in the moment. Which makes it impossible to be present. Which makes it impossible to be curious. Which therefore makes it impossible to be mindful.

Activity: Your Lisa

Okay, so we all have one. Spend the next few minutes writing down all the labels you have for your particular Lisa. Don't overthink this. Just let it rip.

1. If you were really on a tirade, what would you be saying?

_____

_____

_____

_____

_____

Okay, great. Chances are you didn't have a problem coming up with things to write. Now, here's the hard part. Put yourself in your Lisa's shoes for a minute.

2.   What words might he/she use to describe those same behaviors?

_____

_____

_____

_____

_____

Now, one of my pesky know-it-all students (judgment!) remarked the other day, "Wait a minute, I get paid to use and exercise my judgment in the course of my job or when it comes to raising my child. And wouldn't saying that judgment is bad technically be judging judgment?"

These are indeed very good points. (Thank goodness for pesky know-it-alls!) And hence now the very important and subtle distinction between judgment and discernment – two words which are often mistakenly used interchangeably.

Judgment vs. Discernment

Judgment: You're a bad person, and I don't want to spend time with you anymore.

Discernment: I don't agree with some of the actions you take and will therefore distance myself from you to establish boundaries in our relationship.

Judgment: My boss is an idiot. I guess I just have to put up with this crap.

Discernment: While I don't often agree with the decisions that my boss makes, I can agree to disagree.

Or finally, this is for all my mother friends out there who often tell me they feel judged:

Judgment: You're such a bad mother. I can't believe you're not breast feeding!

Discernment: While I have decided to breast feed my child because I feel it is best for my baby, I can see how you might make a different choice and respect your right as a mother to make the best choices you can for your child.

Judgment is typically attached to a statement of worthiness. And if you're struggling with this one, the acid test I often use is one of intention. Is my intention in this situation to be right and/or to make the other person wrong? If your answer to this question is yes, chances are you're making a judgment. If your intention is to carefully and objectively weigh evidence and make the best choice you can for you, chances are you're using discernment.

So, yes, a keen sense of discernment is often what your employer is paying you for. Yes, a keen sense of discernment is a requirement for raising a child. Just be sure to leave the judging to Judge Judy.

Forget, for a second, about all the judgments that we make about other folks. Let's shift the focus now slightly and look at all the judgments that we unconsciously and often mindlessly make about ourselves – judgments we actually mistakenly believe are true.

I know you might find this hard to believe, but for years I truly believed I was selfish and uncaring. Despite the fact that I often did charity work, despite the fact that I had a great many friends who I knew cared deeply about me, despite the fact that I was pursuing a career that was all about helping other people reach their full potential, and even despite the fact that I couldn't bear to watch those gut-wrenching animal cruelty commercials (you know, the ones where they play the sad music and show those pitiful pictures of dogs in a cage), I still believed I was as selfish and uncaring as one of the Kardashian sisters.

Why, you ask? It all boiled down to one limiting belief that I had heard many years ago. And to be honest, I'm not even sure where I heard it. Maybe it was on TV, maybe it was a family member, maybe it was a friend, maybe I read it. Who knows? No matter where I picked it up, it was there. You see, that's how limiting beliefs work. They're subtle, and we gradually absorb a number of them throughout our lives. No one is immune. And the belief you ask? It's one that you may have even heard yourself. Maybe you've even said it yourself (no judgment). "Women who don't have children are selfish and uncaring."

Whether you believe this statement to be true or not, isn't really the point. This statement meets the criteria for and is indeed a judgment. And for years I carried this one around like a sack of sand on my back. It occupied my thoughts and became that running dialogue in the recesses of my mind that often hung over me like a heavy cloud and kept me from showing up as fully present in certain situations. It would often play in my mind like a continuous loop.

The result was that I spent a lot of time and energy trying to prove to myself (and others) that I was neither selfish nor uncaring. Time that could have been much better spent somewhere else. Anywhere else to be precise.

The most interesting point of this entire story is that I had never thought to question this limiting belief in the first place. I had taken it on unconsciously and completely as real. Which brings me back to the topic of mindfulness and the importance of consciously choosing the thoughts we take on. Had I been mindful in the first place, I might have asked myself the following questions right off the bat:

1. Why might this statement be untrue?
2. What is a completely different way of looking at this?

3. Where do I believe this thought comes from?

4. How does this idea fit in with my values?

Hmmmm. Well, hindsight is 20/20, right?

Activity: Reframing Limiting Beliefs

Now it's your turn. What is one belief that you currently hold that is limiting you in some way? If you're struggling coming up with something, think about the things that typically cause you to feel guilt or shame, e.g. I'm a bad mother because, I'm a bad son because . . .

1. My limiting belief is:

_____

_____

_____

_____

_____

2. Why might this statement be untrue?

_____

_____

_____

_____

_____

3. What is a completely different way of looking at this?

_____

_____

_____

_____

_____

4. Where do I believe this thought comes from?

_____

_____

_____

_____

_____

5. How does this idea fit in with my values?

_____

_____

_____

_____

_____

Now, every time that limiting belief comes up, take yourself through these questions. You're guaranteed to feel better every time. And remember, it's not about just running through this check list once. These judgments have been kicking around in your mind for a long time, and many of them are hard wired. The key to this activity is repetition. Practice makes better (no perfect allowed!)

And while we're on the topic of self-judgment, no discussion would be complete without a mention of the sneakiest self-judgment of them all: the Impostor Syndrome.

If you haven't heard about it, you're probably still familiar with it. It's the deep rooted belief that, underneath it all, you're really just a fraud. That somehow you've fooled everyone else into thinking that you're competent, and eventually you're going to be found out. It wasn't all the hard work and dedication that you put in. It was that you got lucky. People helped you. It was a team effort. You couldn't have done it alone. Sound familiar? And while it's a known fact that this affects men as well as women, it does appear to have a stronger hold on high-achieving women.

Don't get me wrong. No one likes a show off. But there is a distinct difference between someone owning their achievements and someone selfishly tooting their own horn all the time.

Self–Compassion: The Antidote to Judgment

I used to keep a journal. And while I've let this practice lapse, a while back I found myself in the house on a rainy day with nothing to do. My fear of boredom got the better of me. I decided to read all of my entries, something I'd never done before. All three hundred and something of them.

At the end of the day when I was finally finished, I put my journal down and sighed. My heart was heavy. The entire book was dripping in self-judgment. On a daily basis, I was beating up on myself over and over again.

"Why am I so emotional? Why am I so impatient? Why am I so scared all the time? Why do I lack confidence? Why can't I be happy? What's wrong with me? If only I could be like Sherri at work. She seems to have it all together."

When I was a little girl, my mother made it a point to remind me constantly to play nicely with others. To treat others the way I would like to be treated. To be sweet and polite when responding to others. To think of others before I thought of myself. And these are all very good things that I did my best to practice as much as possible. And I still do.

But it begs the question, what about the relationship we have with ourselves? Surely this must be just as important as the relationship we have with others? The answer is it's even more important. No doubt you've heard the expression that is phrased in many different ways but goes something like this, "Other people are simply a mirror for what's going on inside you."

A number of years ago, I got bored yet again and changed careers. I went from the very safe and secure world of risk management that I had known for many years, albeit despised, to the unknown and highly ambiguous world of leadership development. This was a strange new world where "it depends" was the standard answer for anything.

The transition was rockier and more dramatic than an episode of *All My Children*. And I was cast in the starring role. Playing opposite me was my boss Alan, another female colleague I referred to as Cat Lady (a crotchety woman who lived alone with a bunch of cats), and the head of our department, a brainy ivory-towered type of guy (you know, the kind that sits in his office all day thinking and never produces anything) whom I referred to as Dr. Doolittle. (Did you get that judgmental pun?)

So, as the story goes, everything was running along just fine and dandy. While all the other characters were busy creating their own dramas, I had managed to avoid getting sucked in for the most part. That is, until about six months into the job, when the shinola literally hit the fan, and a project I was responsible for delivering didn't go oh so well. Dr. Doolittle, Cat Lady, and Alan were not impressed.

And, frankly, neither was I. Always having been the perfectionist type of person who prided herself on getting perfect grades and delivering perfect work products, I was devastated for months on end. I kept thinking to myself, "Why all the drama? Say you're sorry, and move on. Correct the mistake, and get over it."

But I had never failed at anything in life up to that point. I had won all the awards, had done everything right. The shame was unbearable. I came very close to throwing in the towel and running off to join the circus as the tall lady. (I'm six foot one in case I haven't mentioned that already.)

But I stayed. And my inability to forgive myself and show myself a little compassion for what had happened turned my department into a full blown torture chamber. Alan, Cat Lady, and Dr. Doolittle were no longer just silly slapstick characters. They were my persecutors who met in secret regularly to plan my demise. They were judging every word I said. They were looking at me in every meeting with contempt. They were plotting to fire me. To take away my responsibility. To publicly humiliate me in front of the entire HR department.

None of this happened by the way. And truth be told, I'm sure Dr. Doolittle was too busy trying to figure out how to work the coffee machine to give the matter much more thought. Cat Lady, in between her crotchety tirades, was occupied in the time-consuming, never-ending task of cleaning cat fur off her sweater. And Alan, if you were wondering, was too busy trying to look important and an essential member of the team to take much notice anyway.

A few months later, I was sitting at home, wallowing in my frustration and fear, and I had a revelation. I grabbed a sheet of paper and drew a vertical line down the middle. At the top of the left hand column, I wrote "I AM NOT." At the top of the right hand column, I wrote "I AM. And then I started writing. When I finally looked up, this is what I had created.

I AM NOT	I AM
At fault	Powerful
Guilty	Passionate
Unloving	Brave
Unworthy	Innovator
Inadequate	Fun
Defined by others	Bullet-proof
My job title	Compassionate
Lazy	Balanced
Angry	Committed

And then I realized something. I could either live on the left hand side of the page, or I could live on the right. The choice was mine really. Sound familiar? (Hint: Think circle.) I could also see possibility. And with that came a feeling of power and freedom.

Back at work, the terrible trio was still there, but something in me had shifted. They were no longer the cruel and evil people responsible for my demise. Granted, they weren't angels either. But as annoying and obnoxious as they could be, they just were. The compassion I had shown myself I extended to them. Because, at the end of the day, that's how self-compassion works. Once you give some to yourself, you don't feel the need to be right all the time. You're right with yourself, and that's what matters.

Activity: What Labels Do I Choose?

Quid pro quo. I'm sure you sensed it would be your turn next. Here's your sheet of paper. Get cracking.

I AM NOT	I AM

1. How does focusing on the I AM side make you feel?

_____

_____

_____

_____

_____

2. When you are feeling this way, what possibilities does this open up for you?

_____

_____

_____

_____

_____

Okay, enough about you. Now back to me.

So maybe you're thinking everything was just peachy keen after I did that exercise for myself. I was the queen of self-compassion, and all judgment disappeared, and I lived from that point onward in a state of curious bliss. Not exactly.

The day after I finished writing this chapter, I missed a call from my friend Mary. I listened to the message and, as I did, I was enveloped by a strong feeling of resentment and anger. Or to be more precise, I blew my top. I slammed the phone down and was so mad I could spit. Selfish, inconsiderate, and yet another person I needed to put on my shinola list.

I had been avoiding Mary for quite some time. From my perspective, our relationship had devolved into a perpetual coaching session where, every time we met, I was forced to sit and listen to her talk about her favorite subject – her. Perhaps it was the soon to be ex-husband. Or maybe it was the new boyfriend. Never mind the fact that I had unconsciously encouraged the situation, been an active participant in it, and never expressed how I really felt. On the shinola list she went.

But there was a slight problem. There was no more room on the list. In fact, over the past six months, the list had gotten really full. It included a long list of colleagues, family members, and friends I was avoiding for certain reasons. My life was getting narrower and narrower. The realization was a sobering and highly ironic one, if I do say so myself. And then the Impostor Syndrome kicked in.

> *"How can this be, the Irreverent Guru of Mindfulness that I am?*
> *I've just finished writing an entire chapter on judgment! I'm*
> *the worst judger of them all! What's wrong with me? I'm such*
> *a fraud."*

A bucket of ice cream later, when the dust had settled and I was in the midst of my sugar coma, I asked myself a different, more empowering question. How well is that list really serving you? And I was filled with a burning desire to get rid of it. In a crazed frenzy, I dropped everything I was doing and spent all day (remember, it was a long list) contacting everyone on my shinola list via any and all possible methods. I was a woman on a mission. It felt good. Liberating. I had found peace. And then I realized there was one final person left on the list where I needed to soften my heart the most.

Six months before I started writing this book, I started my own business. Exciting, yes. Challenging, yes. And also a great opportunity to judge myself and beat myself up on a regular basis.

"If I wasn't so lazy maybe I'd be doing more business development. You don't know anything about how to market on social media, you've never been the technical type.

Why can't you be more like Marie Forleo? She's got a huge following.

You're never going to get on Oprah's Super Soul Sunday at the rate you're going.

You're just a hack."

And so on and so on. Remember that quote – other people are just a mirror for how you're feeling about yourself? And so I dragged out my self-compassion audio series, and I actually managed to listen this time.

Which brings me back to the definition of mindfulness once again. Particularly the word practice. Practice makes better (remember, no perfect allowed!).

In summary:

- We all make judgments; our minds are often judgment-making machines. The key is to be aware of it.
- Suspending judgment makes space for possibility.
- Judgment is typically associated with a statement of worthiness. The acid test is intention. Is it my intent to be right in this situation and/or to make the other person wrong?
- Judgment should not be confused with discernment, which is the act of carefully weighing evidence and making an objective choice.
- When you find yourself blocked by self-judgment, remember the check list! Why might this statement be untrue? What is a completely different way of looking at this? Where do I believe this thought comes from? How does this idea fit in with my values?
- Self-compassion is the antidote to judgment. Practice it every day. It's just what the doctor ordered.
- The relationships we have with other people are typically a mirror for the one we have with ourselves. When you're feeling a lot of friction, look inwards.

So now we've tackled judgment, one of the most important mindfulness blocks. And if you're wondering what a mindfulness block is, onward ho, fearless reader. In the next chapter, we take a deeper dive into all of the other distractions, such as fear and anxiety, that keep us from being the mindfulness gurus we were born to be.

Chapter 4

Mindfulness Blocks:

Those Pesky Little Things That Get in the Way of Our Zen

". . . feelings like disappointment, embarrassment, irritation, resentment, anger, jealousy, and fear, instead of being bad news, are actually very clear moments that teach us where it is that we're holding back. They teach us to perk up and lean in when we feel we'd rather collapse and back away. They're like messengers that show us, with terrifying clarity, exactly where we're stuck. This very moment is the perfect teacher, and, lucky for us, it's with us wherever we are."

~ Pema Chödrön, When Things Fall Apart: Heart Advice for Difficult Times

In this chapter:

- Shelley's MindLESS Moment
- Definition of a Mindfulness Block
- Shelley's Many Mindfulness Blocks
- Activity: Draw Your Mindfulness Block (yes, you read that right!)
- A Stroke of Insight
- The Case of the Negative Networker

- Activity: Name That Mindfulness Block
- Activity: Bust Your Mindfulness Block!!!

On July 4, 2013, I was where I normally am – the annual 4th of July picnic in St. John, Texas. Chances are you haven't heard of it. The town consists of a church, and that's basically it. I'm not sure if there's even a post office, but hey ho, who needs the mail when you've got beer in the blistering heat? Anyway, there I was, in the blazing Texas sun, the humidity steadily approaching 100%, desperately seeking shade under the one pavilion and ginormous fan that the church recreation center provided.

Three Lone Star Lights later (a girl gets thirsty in all that heat), I spied my aunt and uncle, who were busy corralling folks into the un-air-conditioned dining hall for the lightest of German-inspired meals – fried chicken, sausage, and sauerkraut. I gave them a friendly wave in consideration of the fact that they are the reason I attend each year. It's their church after all. And then I set off to partake in the drama and pageantry of the auction. Who doesn't love an $80 jar of pickles? At least they're homemade, or so I've been told.

It was there that I ran into my cousin Heather. And the day pretty much went downhill after that. I'll admit I wasn't looking forward to the encounter. My fiancé and I had recently gotten engaged, and we weren't exactly the traditional types when it came to planning our big day. No church, no priest, and no fried chicken on our agenda. And while I did my best to steer the conversation away from this particular topic, it eventually reared its ugly head.

"So you're having a private ceremony? Does that mean we're not invited?"

Oh, no. Here we go . . . And then the train really went off the track. The meltdown was starting. I could feel my resentment and anger bubbling up throughout the conversation. Heather was judging me – I just knew it!

"Who does she think she is? What gives her the right? Just because she had the picture-perfect, 400-person wedding doesn't mean that everyone has to do it that way, right? That preachy, sanctimonious, condescending, you-know-what!"

(Not that I was being the slightest bit judgmental, the Irreverent Guru of Mindfulness that I am.)

Actually, my mind had left the conversation completely. I was no longer hearing anything she had to say. I was now enveloped in a paralyzing wave of guilt and shame.

"Maybe she's right. How could I do this to my family?

What's wrong with me?"

But enough insight into my bizarre family life for now, let's get on with the topic at hand. And to do so we'll start at the very beginning by answering the following excellent question, "What the heck is a mindfulness block?"

Remember the definition of mindfulness?

Definition of mindfulness: The practice of focusing awareness on the present moment non-judgmentally.

So, with that said, a mindfulness block really is, quite simply, something that keeps us from being in the present moment. My favorite way of thinking about it is it's something that effectively "hijacks" us out of the present moment. Or, in other words, it's a persistent thought or feeling that reduces awareness of the present moment.

So back to the saga of me and my dear cuz. It would be fair to say that my feelings and emotions took over during that fateful conversation. So much so that I was tuned into the running dialogue in my head instead of the dialogue I was having with her. My judgment rose and rose and then rose some more, which made it impossible for me to be curious, listen to her perspective, or ask clarifying questions. It would be fair to say that it wasn't my proudest or most mindful moment.

Now, it would have been one thing if I had just left it alone at that point. If I had just gone on about my business and the task of planning my wedding. Forgive and forget. C'est la vie! But, oh no, that's not how mindfulness blocks typically work. Once you get hijacked the first time, the thought or feeling typically comes back over and over and over again to torture you. Just imagine your least favorite song playing at full blast all day long on a continuous loop. (Pour some sugar on me! Pour some sugar on me! Pour some sugar on me! Oh my god kill me now . . .) And this gets super annoying, because you effectively end up reliving the experience many, many times and feeling a countless number of less than helpful emotions many, many times.

For example, I would think of the situation and feel that initial guilt and shame, that feeling that I had done something bad and wronged my family. Then anger would start to rear its ugly head.

"This isn't my problem. It's her problem. How dare she make me feel like that!"

Cue my resentment and judgment that typically would follow my anger to enter stage left and make their appearance.

"That sanctimonious nit-wit. She always thinks she knows best!"

Which would eventually lead to sadness.

"We used to be like sisters. I can't believe our relationship has devolved into this!"

Which would typically then lead to me feeling guilty and ashamed again for the role I had played in the demise of our relationship.

"I shouldn't have said this. I shouldn't have said that."

It was one long continuous loop of emotional doom, where shame was ultimately at the root of it all.

What's really interesting about this phenomenon is that Ed and his mystical mindfulness monk friends knew all about this common human experience ages ago. They knew it so well that they actually invented a term which describes this exact experience. It's called "shenpa," which in Tibetan literally means "to get hooked."

Even the calm, serene, mystical mindfulness monk occasionally gets hooked. Who would have thought? Maybe someone stole his favorite meditation mat again.

We usually experience many different mindfulness blocks during a typical day, and those blocks can take the form of any of the following:

Shelley's Many Mindfulness Blocks*

Anger	Fear	Rejection
Anxiety	Frustration	Resentment
Apathy	Greed	Resignation
Apprehension	Guilt	Resistance
Blame	Helplessness	Restlessness
Boredom	Hopelessness	Sadness
Confusion	Insecurity	Self-consciousness
Defiance	Intimidation	Scepticism
Disappointment	Jealousy	Shame
Distrust	Judgment	Stress
Embarrassment	Loneliness	Unworthiness
Emptiness	Overwhelm	Victimhood
Entitlement	Perfectionism	Worry

*Perfectionist Disclaimer: Please note that this list is not all-inclusive. However, it is in perfectionistic alphabetical order for your convenience!

If you read the list quickly, it sounds like the side effects from one of those annoying prescription drug commercials. But take a good long look, and you may notice something about this list. Go ahead, look. I'll wait . . . Doo dee doo dee doo . . .

What do all of these things have in common? If, after careful scrutiny, you're wondering why all of these blocks look like emotions, it's because they are.

During a typical day, we experience many of these emotions, often unconsciously. I'm happily writing away, the words are flowing, I can feel the writing muse taking hold. Eureka! And then suddenly my thoughts are hijacked by those pesky, nagging feelings of stress, overwhelm, and perhaps even fear. I get that sinking feeling in my stomach. My chest starts to feel tight. And my thoughts suddenly veer off in another direction.

"Oh my God, I haven't found a publisher yet. How on earth am I going to market this book? Should I have a launch party? All the big important writers have launch parties. How does one organize a launch party? Uggggh . . . too much to think about. I'm almost finished, and I haven't figured out that trick for making your book a bestseller on Amazon. What if no one reads it? What if people think it sucks, and I become a laughing stock?"

And suddenly the muse is gone. And for the life of me I still can't figure out where she went.

Activity: Draw Your Mindfulness Block

Step 1: Think of one situation that is currently causing you to feel blocked. It could be a particular person that triggers it, e.g. your equivalent of the pesky cousin (we all have one!). It could also be a particular situation that tends to trigger you, e.g. work deadlines that are looming. Got it? Good.

Step 2: Using the space below, I want you to draw a picture of this block. Yes, you read me right. I want you to *draw* a picture of the block.

Step 3: Once you've finished the drawing, I want you to label it with the mindfulness block emotion that best describes what is going on, e.g. shame, guilt, judgment, anger. Don't forget there could be a number of emotions firing off in your emotional soup. Remember my emotional loop of doom? Think about the one feeling that is the root emotion. It's important to get clarity on this because we will work with it later.

Perfectionist Disclaimer: There is no right or wrong drawing. Unleash your inner artist! Flex that creative muscle. It could look like anything. When I did this for myself, I ended up with a tall, blonde version of Nathaniel Hawthorne's Hester Prynne from the *Scarlet Letter* standing up on a podium holding a sign that said "Shame!" while her jeering family threw rotten tomatoes at her. (An amazing work of art if I do say so myself.)

Or if Hawthorne doesn't float your boat, one of my students illustrated her feeling of overwhelm with a drawing of a sink full of dirty dishes in a cluttered kitchen. It looked so real, I took one look, and it transported me back to my lazy college days in an instant. Now that's talent.

Your Mindfulness Block Drawing

(Yes, I'm serious. I want you to draw it right here in the book because otherwise you won't do it. You know you won't.)

All right, enough time spent imitating Picasso.

So what about all those other distractions in life besides our emotions? You know, things like our smartphones or our kids or our pesky mother-in-law. You know, the things that keep us from being – wait for it – mindful. Wouldn't these things also be mindfulness blocks? And in order to answer that excellent question, let's go back to the definition of a mindfulness block yet again:

Mindfulness Block: A persistent thought or feeling that reduces awareness of the present moment

Distractions are a part of life. No matter how hard you may try to control them, they will always be there. The trick is how we manage them. In a later chapter, we'll look at strategies for managing one of our most common distractions and a significant block to our mindfulness, technology. The chapter includes some excellent and thought-provoking commentary about how to use that most necessary of today's blessings as well as a curse, the smartphone.

In my experience (and I think the Eds of the world would agree), the biggest cause of mindlessness is our own mind, which is often jumbled up and chock full of the numerous problems and clutter we manage to create for ourselves. So it makes sense to get our own house in order first before we start worrying how to manage Dear Mother-in-Law. The added benefit of beginning with our own personal housecleaning is that a clearer mind can better manage all those other pesky life distractions coming at us over which we have far less, if any control. All this to say, clearing our mindfulness blocks is really an inside job.

Now, I wouldn't blame you for thinking at this point, "Okay, fine. I can see how we are often our worst enemy after all. But wait a second, Shelley. Are you saying I'm not supposed to have emotions now? What about all the fuss about emotional intelligence? EI was like the biggest buzzword ever to grace the pages of *Harvard Business Review*. What about all those self-help gurus who are always saying silly things like you need to feel your feelings?"

And you would be exactly right, because I am NOT saying you aren't supposed to have emotions or feel those emotions. Let me give you an example to clarify what I mean about emotions.

Think about your favorite sad movie. Take a few minutes right now. Put down the book and let yourself get immersed with the story and the characters. Go ahead. I'll wait . . . Doo dee doo dee doo . . .

Now, why do we watch a sad movie? To feel better about our lives when we're feeling down and out?

No.

To revel in someone else's misfortune?

Nice try, but no.

The answer is we watch a sad movie TO FEEL. Emotions are the elixir of life. They add depth and dimension to our human experience.

However, there is a distinct difference between an emotion that arises spontaneously out of the present moment and the continuous loop sagas we all allow ourselves to be hijacked by over and over and over again. For example, there is the spontaneous emotion of grief as you watch your beloved Fluffy pass on to the other side. And then there is the continuous loop saga of second-guessing yourself and obsessing about whether you euthanized Fluffy too soon or too late. Do you see the difference? More importantly, do you FEEL the difference?

A number of years back, a woman named Jill Bolte Taylor, an award-winning neuroscientist, had a stroke. What's interesting about this stroke is that it shut down only half of her brain – the part of the brain that's responsible for cognitive thought, to be precise. What's even more interesting about this experience is that the effect was she lived entirely in the present moment.

Once Jill had recovered, she went on to call this unfortunate event her "stroke of insight" and demonstrated scientifically that emotions really only last about 90 seconds. That's it. 90 seconds. The rest of the time we're stuck there it's a choice. Sometimes it may be the right choice. It would be hard to imagine grieving a total of only 90 seconds for poor Fluffy. But more often than not, when we get stuck in an emotion, it's an unconscious choice that doesn't serve us very well.

So how do you get unstuck from this emotional soup when it is indeed not serving you? In order to unpick this, let's think about emotions for a moment. We frequently give emotions a lot of stature. They can be powerful, come on when we least expect them, overwhelm us, and even cause us to make fools of ourselves in public. (Not that this has ever happened to yours truly. I always managed to leg it to the loo to cry it out in secret just in the nick of time.)

But what is an emotion really? If you think about it long and hard enough and spend enough time with the Eds of this world or even on Google, you'll probably arrive at the following widely-accepted definition:

An emotion is a physical reaction in the body to a thought.

That's it. This simple phrase is ultimately all an emotion really is.

So, all this to say that, in order to have an emotion, there has to be an underlying thought. Doesn't matter if you're even aware of it. It's there, hiding like the bad smell of that moldy French brie you forgot in the fridge. Which begs yet another interesting and empowering question – "If I could change the thought, could I change the emotion?"

To which the answer is a resounding yes.

A few years back in my work as a leadership development guru, I stumbled across a very interesting tool rooted in cognitive behavioral therapy that I now use all the time in my work as a coach. And because I am the super generous and altruistic person that I am, I'm even going to share it with you. I call it the Thought–Feeling–Action Framework, and it works like this:

"Okay, networking. I know I have to do this for my business. God, I really hate networking. When I think of networking, I always think of a used car salesman trying to make a quick buck. I feel fake, I feel sleazy. Yuck. Then I do one of two things. One, I go to the networking event but avoid talking about myself and my business because I don't want to feel sleazy or appear that I'm just out to make a quick sale. Or two, I just don't go at all."

You may have guessed that the above tirade used to be one of my favorite mindfulness blocks. And while a very interesting diatribe, not super helpful when you've recently started a business. Using the Thought–Feeling–Action Framework, here's a brief recap of what was going on for me:

Thought: Networking is phony
Feeling: Disgust
Action: Avoidance of networking

(The Case of the Negative Networker to be continued. Stick with me.)

Activity: Name That Mindfulness Block

If you're old enough, you may remember that tired game show, *Name That Tune*. I myself have fond and even vivid memories of watching the old color TV at my grandmother's house, the bowl of cheesy Cheetos overflowing and staining the rug, and the smell of moth balls in the air. But I digress.

Now it's time to name that mindfulness block! Think back to the picture you just drew and the emotion you used to label your block. Remember how I mentioned it was important to identify the root emotion? Fill out the following for your block:

Thought: _____

Feeling: (the label you used on your drawing, the root emotion)

Action: _____

Perfectionist Disclaimer: It's not about exactly nailing the thought word for word. You're looking to capture the essence of it. This may take a little time and a little digging. You'll know you've gotten it when you think the thought, and the feeling starts to arise.

Great. You've identified your block. Now back to me and the Case of the Negative Networker. Since I was aware I was blocked with respect to networking (the Irreverent Guru of Mindfulness that I am), I decided to ask myself a few questions:

1. How do I want to show up instead?

2. What would I need to **feel** in order to show up that way?

3. What would I therefore need to **think** in order to feel that way?

   "Okay, so this isn't working for me. I know something needs to change. So how do I want to show up in the future? I want to show up at these events and confidently speak about who I am and how I can help people.

   So if I want to show up speaking confidently about who I am and how I can help people, how would I need to feel in order to do that? I'd need to feel excited and energized about the opportunity to network.

   Then what would I need to think in order to make me really feel excited and energized about networking? Hmmm ... okay, surely the opposite of this statement will work. Networking isn't phony? Nope, that's not it. When I think that, I don't feel any different because I really don't believe it.

   Let's try again ... networking is an opportunity for me to enhance my business. That sounds better, and while it may very well be true, it still doesn't work. It still feels really self-serving. Why is that? Maybe I'm thinking about networking from the perspective of what I can get. What about if I thought about networking in terms of what I can give to others? Hmmmm ...

that's interesting. I like to give. I like to help people. That's why I got into this business in the first place.

Okay, so maybe networking is an opportunity for me to find folks who can benefit from my skills and talents. Wow. When I think that, I really start to feel different. By George, I think I've got it!"

Or, in other words:

Thought: Networking is an opportunity to serve; it's all about what I can give.

Feeling: Excited

Action: Confident networking

I want you to notice a few things about that inner dialogue of mine. One, the beauty of the Thought–Feeling–Action Framework is that I could have started with the feeling instead of the action. What do I want to feel instead? How would I show up if I felt that way? If I was showing up that way, what would I be thinking? I also could have started with the thought. No matter where I start, I end up in exactly the same place. This is useful because it's often easier to identify the action or the feeling first instead of the underlying thought.

Two, it sometimes takes a number of tries to figure out the right thought that's going to work to reframe the block. If the first try doesn't work, then try again. And again and again. Keep trying. You'll know it's working when you actually start to feel the emotion you're targeting. You'll start to feel a shift. This is a great sensory check to determine whether or not you are on the right track.

Three, you can't trick yourself with words. I repeat, you CANNOT trick yourself with words. In my experience, exercises like this often get marginalized because of a belief that this is a bait and switch you do on yourself. Notice that I tried that tactic first. If I feel networking is phony, then I'll just tell myself networking isn't phony. Wrong. You have to do the work. There is no free lunch, muchachos.

Finally, if you've tried and tried and aren't getting anywhere, go back to the beginning and your drawing. Chances are you haven't nailed the root emotion. This is why identifying it accurately is so important in the first place. (This is also why many self-help gurus make such a fuss about the topic of emotional intelligence.)

At the end of the day, emotional intelligence is just a fancy way of saying "awareness" or "mindfulness." Awareness of the emotions we're experiencing, the impact they have on us, and the impact they have on others. That's it. (You should thank me. I just saved you a lot of time and effort. Books on emotional intelligence tend to be long reads.) So, in order to bust a mindfulness block, you've got to correctly identify the root emotion itself. Only then can you really get to the bottom of the block.

Think back to the example of me and my dear cuz. I stayed stuck for so long because I focused on the anger I felt towards her.

Thought: That mean and nasty you-know-what cuz!

Feeling: Anger

Action: Avoidance of cuz

When I dug a little deeper, I realized it really had nothing to do with her. It was the shame I felt about going against the proverbial grain and doing something I had been taught was wrong. Here's what was really going on:

Thought: I did something bad.

Feeling: Shame

Action: Pick a fight with cuz

Activity: Bust Your Mindfulness Block!!!

Okay, so now it's your turn to take a crack at your mindfulness block. Decide where you want to start first. Any of the three (thought, feeling, action) will work. Then ask yourself the three simple questions:

1. How do I want to _____ instead?

2. What would I need to _____ in order to _____ that way?

3. What would I therefore need to _____ in order to

_____ that way?

Now that you've asked yourself these three handy-dandy questions, you're ready to write your new thought, feeling and action:

New Thought: _____

_____

New Feeling: _____

_____

New Action: _____

_____

Now that you've got your new thought, feeling, and action, it's important to practice it. Yep, that's right. Yet again practice makes better. Unfortunately, this doesn't work like one of David Copperfield's slick magic tricks. Poof! Old thought, feeling, and action gone forever!

Chances are the old thought, feeling, and action were ingrained for quite a while in that continuous loop of doom. They most likely will try to sneak back into your consciousness from time to time. When you recognize that happening, immediately replace them with the new thought, feeling, and action.

And here's the most important part. No judgment! There is absolutely no sense in beating yourself up if you notice the loop is back. All it does is serve to compound the problem by introducing a whole new slew of mindfulness blocks into the mix, such as self-anger, frustration, disappointment, and/or blame. Remember, you're striving for excellence, not perfection.

"(Your name), Rome wasn't built in a day."

"(Your name), it's the journey that counts, not the destination."

"(Your name), progress not perfection."

Or use whatever well-intentioned cliché tends to work for you in these situations.

In summary:

- A mindfulness block is a persistent thought or feeling that reduces awareness of the present moment. Think of it simply as something that hooks or hijacks you out of the present moment.
- Each day we experience many mindfulness blocks. Don't worry. It's perfectly normal and part of the human experience.
- Distractions are distractions, and they will always be there. Mindfulness blocks are an inside job.

- Emotions are a physical reaction in the body to a thought.

- Emotional intelligence is just a fancy word for awareness or mindfulness – awareness of the emotions we're experiencing, the impact they have on us, and the impact they have on others.

- When you recognize that you're blocked, try to isolate the root emotion, e.g. shame, anger, resentment, sadness.

- Remember to name your block! What is the underlying thought, feeling, and action you are experiencing?

- When busting your block, remember the three questions: How do I want to act instead? What would I need to **feel** in order to act that way? What would I therefore need to **think** in order to feel that way?

- Once you have your new thought, feeling, and action, it's time to practice. The old thought, feeling, and action will come back at some point. Recognize, reframe, replace, and move on.

Now that you're armed with a special tool for busting those pesky mindfulness blocks, we're going to shift focus slightly and look at an age-old practice that also aids in clarity of thought – meditation. In the next chapter, I'm going to take on the epic task of teaching an old dog a new trick. Why? Because most of what we believe to be true about the practice of meditation is completely wrong. (And, yes, I just called you an old dog.)

Chapter 5

Ommmmmmm, What Is It Really?

Demystifying Meditation

"In meditation we discover our inherent restlessness. Sometimes we get up and leave. Sometimes we sit there, but our bodies wiggle and squirm, and our minds go far away. This can be so uncomfortable that we feel it's impossible to stay. Yet this feeling can teach us not just about ourselves but what it is to be human . . . we really don't want to stay with the nakedness of our present experience. It goes against the grain to stay present."

~ Pema Chödrön, The Places That Scare You: A Guide to Fearlessness in Difficult Times

(And, yes, I know that's two Pema quotes in a row.)

In this chapter:

- The Secret to Meditation
- The Purpose of Meditation
- Meditation Quiz #1
- The Goal of Meditation
- 10 Myths About Meditation

- Meditation Quiz #2
- Activity: Increase Your Meditation Moments

Let's start the exploration of practical ways to develop a mindfulness regimen with the most misunderstood. Tackle the biggest mountain first I always say.

If you're like most folks, you've probably heard of meditation. Maybe you've even thought about trying it. Or maybe you went the whole hog and really gave it a go. You went down to Whole Foods and bought real incense from India, candles, and maybe even one of those cheap, plastic Buddha statues. (Why not? It looks really Zen, and it was on sale after all.) The whole enchilada as we Texans say.

You managed to sneak to a quiet corner of your house, sat down on the floor, and lit the candles and the incense. (Wow! this stuff really is smelly. I hope it doesn't catch the house on fire.) You closed your eyes, took a few deep cleansing breaths, focused your attention on your third eye like that Cosmo magazine article told you to do and then felt . . . a massive wave of disappointment. Somehow it just didn't feel like you were doing it right. Sigh. Buddha is now living out his days as a highly functional paperweight or a chew toy for Fluffy the dog.

Have no fear. Starting a meditation practice can often feel just like that, like it did for me when I started.

The secret to meditating is getting rid of all the garbage we carry around in our heads about what it's supposed to look and feel like. And don't tell me you don't have any garbage! Trust me, you do. It may have been from something you saw on *Oprah* or in that other highly educational article you read in *Cosmo* while you were at the nail salon getting a pedicure.

Whatever it was, I'm going to ask you to suspend your judgment (also a great mindfulness practice, remember?) and consider that meditation doesn't have to look like anything at all. That's why this chapter is not so much dedicated to the how of meditating, but rather to debunking the myths we believe about it that keep us from getting up on that trusty horse and trying it in the first place.

Which brings me back to the point of meditation. It might be somewhat helpful if I explained why you should even bother in the first place. Meditation is a way of focusing your attention so you start to sense the space between your thoughts. That's it. It's not about zoning out or seeing cool colors or visions of unicorns and butterflies. After all, there are plenty of other substances to help you with all that.

The reason it's a mindfulness practice is that you start to become more aware of the thoughts that you're thinking. And that is a really important thing, considering that we think, on average, about 10,000 thoughts a day. It hurts my brain to think that I can even think 10,000 thoughts a day! (Hopefully that made sense.) Some folks' estimates are even higher.

When I first heard that statistic I was floored. But the more I thought about it, the more I started to realize how true it was. Have you ever found your mind wandering and then tried to link the final thought back to where you started? Try it sometime. It's a really interesting trip (even without the psychedelic substances).

"Okay, so mindfulness and meditation, let's see.

Those tulips on my window sill are so beautiful. They remind me of the first time my husband gave me tulips.

That was when we lived in that condo in Houston.

Wow, I really liked that condo, except for that one time we had rats in the attic.

I hate rats.

Houston has so many rats. I wonder why, maybe it's because it's so humid?

Those rats were attracted to that grapefruit tree Old Lady Neva had in her yard behind our condo.

Oh wait, the condo.

I wonder if the present owners have renovated it?

That was such a bumpy sale. That realtor we used was horrible.

Who was it that recommended her? Maybe it was Trish?

I wonder if Trish still lives two doors down?

Trish was so much fun.

I miss Trish.

We used to sit for hours at the bar at Lupe Tortilla eating queso.

Ummmmm . . . it's been ages since I've had queso.

I wish I had some right now."

And that explains how that day of writing got derailed to the Mexican restaurant around the corner from my house. It also demonstrates how the mind is the equivalent of that annoying family member we all have, aka crazy Aunt Flo, who rambles on and on and on and never shuts up.

So with all of these thoughts, when does a person just have time to, you know, just be? Maybe take a rest? Take a break? The answer is not very often.

Think back to the dog track I mentioned earlier. Your mind is always racing like the dog chasing the mechanical rabbit around the track. And you're typically focused on one of two things: the past, thinking about what happened and wishing it could have been different; or the future, thinking and often feeling anxious about what's to come. That next phone call, email, appointment, project. Whatever it is, you fill in the blank.

I talk about this a lot when I teach yoga. We never are where we are. Meditation is a practice in bringing you back to the present moment. Over and over and over and over again. And, in case you've forgotten, the present moment is the only place where true happiness lies.

Here's another way of looking at the benefit of meditation. Have you ever been in a particularly tricky situation, maybe at work or at home, when your emotions got the better of you? You know, one of those days when, like me, you've also had to "leg it to the loo" so to speak so you can scream and bang on the toilet stall doors and no one will be the wiser?

What's even worse than the situation itself are those patronizing folks that say in their all-knowing, singsongy tone of voice things like, "You're in control of your emotions." Or "Respond, don't react." I have always hated those people because the problem I had with that advice was how the heck am I supposed to do that? I mean, if it were that easy, I wouldn't be screaming my guts out in the bathroom and banging on the toilet stall doors, would I?

Well, I'm a practical person, and the bottom line is that meditation works where this stuff is concerned. Over time, you will find that you just don't get as agitated about these things anymore. "How can this be?" you ask. Because you realize the thought that is driving you nuts is just a thought. You'll have another 9,999 that day, so why get all bent out of shape over this one?

Okay, enough about the benefits of meditation. I think you probably get it by now. As I mentioned before, the focus of this chapter is demystifying meditation, so let's get on to debunking those myths. In order to do this, I'm enlisting the help of Mr. Meditation himself, Deepak Chopra. On our quest for meditation truth, we will start with his seven myths since it's as good a place as any. And we'll finish up with yours truly's three myths to arrive at an easy-to-remember number of ten things not to believe about meditation.

But first I want you to take the following quiz, which will provide a useful starting point for our discussions.

Meditation Quiz #1

Rate how much you agree with the following statements on a scale of 1 to 10, with 1 indicating you don't agree whatsoever with the statement and 10 indicating you completely agree.

Meditation is difficult.

    1   2   3   4   5   6   7   8   9   10

You have to quiet your mind to have a successful meditation practice.

    1   2   3   4   5   6   7   8   9   10

It takes years of dedicated practice to receive any benefits from meditation.

    1   2   3   4   5   6   7   8   9   10

Meditation is escapism.

    1   2   3   4   5   6   7   8   9   10

I don't have enough time to meditate.

    1   2   3   4   5   6   7   8   9   10

Meditation is a spiritual or religious practice.

    1   2   3   4   5   6   7   8   9   10

I'm supposed to have transcendent experiences in meditation.

    1   2   3   4   5   6   7   8   9   10

Finished? Great. By the way, all of these statements are myths according to Mr. Meditation, Dr. Deepak Chopra (www.chopra.com/ccl/7-myths-of-meditation). Yours truly happens to agree with him. So now you have a nice, handy dandy diagnostic tool for where you might need to focus your meditation myth debunking efforts. Let's tackle the first couple of myths at the same time.

Myth #1: Meditation is difficult.

AND

Myth #2: You have to quiet your mind in order to have a successful meditation practice.

Think back to what I said earlier in this chapter. We think approximately 10,000 thoughts per day. Imagine that our untamed mind is like a swiftly moving river, the thoughts rushing one after the other as fast as they can. Imagine trying to build a dam by hand to contain that river. Good luck. I don't care how hard you try or how many beavers you enlist, it's an impossible feat. So is trying to quiet your mind and not think anything at all. It's similar to trying to roll an extremely large and heavy boulder up a very steep hill. (No wonder Sisyphus was so tired.) No wonder so many folks think meditation is difficult! It's downright impossible if you believe you're supposed to completely quiet that rushing river of thoughts.

The goal of meditation is simply to observe the space between your thoughts. When you find your mind wandering, just bring it back to the present moment. When it starts to wander again like Fluffy the dog in pursuit of that pesky squirrel, no problemo. Kindly bring it back again. Come back, Fluffy, come back! This is a dance that goes on and on when we meditate. Where we tend to get stuck and start to view the practice as difficult is when we start this:

"I shouldn't be thinking right now, I should be meditating. I'm such a bad meditator. I'm horrible at this. I don't have the patience. Why did I think I could do this? This is stupid. I'm stupid. I can't believe I tried this! I can't believe I spent five whole dollars on that cheap, plastic Buddha statue. This incense smells like crap. Who was I kidding anyway?!"

Observing your thoughts means not judging them. We spend so much time labeling things good, bad, right, wrong. It's exhausting. I often start off any meditation I do with an intention to be compassionate with myself. If I meditate for a half hour and the entire time my mind is running on and on like crazy Aunt Flo, no biggie. It's the simple practice of meditating that matters, not the outcome.

Myth #3: It takes years of dedicated practice to receive any benefits from meditation.

Enter Ed, stage left. Remember Ed, The Mystical Mindfulness Monk?

"I bet Ed's really good at meditation. He's a monk, so he should be. I bet he's trained for years and years and learned lots of special, fancy monk things. Meditation is complicated and tricky. I'm a normal person with a busy life. I haven't trained. I can't devote more than a few minutes a day. Meditation is for people like Ed, not for people that live in the real world."

I often tell students, if two minutes a day is all you have, two minutes a day works. It's a marathon folks, not a sprint. The trick is consistency not perfection.

Myth #4: Meditation is escapism.

This one was my Achilles heel, being a corporate gal. Often people associate meditation with the stereotypical woo-woo hippie that is completely out of touch with reality and the real world. (Don't tell me you haven't thought it at least once!) You know, those people with crystals that wear flowy clothes. They are vegan or at least gluten-free. They live in one of those eco houses that they built by hand out of a shipping crate using primitive tools and solar energy. They just can't hack living in the real world so they have to escape. You think to yourself, "Well, life would be just peachy for me too if I didn't have any responsibilities and could just run off to a commune and live with the animals in the forest. Free love, right?"

Say what you want, but the reality is that all people, from an infinite variety of backgrounds and walks of life, meditate. Oprah meditates and runs one of the most successful broadcasting companies in the world. Billionaire Ray Dalio, who runs the Bridgewater hedge fund, credits meditation with his success. Rupert Murdoch the media mogul? Yep, him too.

Myth #5: I don't have enough time to meditate.

When I was developing the course content for the mindfulness program I teach at the University of Texas at Austin, I found myself getting up in the morning and moving straight to my computer. "Too much to do, too much to do," I would think. "I'll meditate later," I would say to myself.

One day the great irony of what I was doing hit me like a frying pan straight to my face – avoiding practicing mindfulness to create a course on practicing mindfulness. I started meditating again that same day. Practice makes better after all.

As I said before, if two minutes is all you have, then two minutes is all you have. It's amazing what a difference even two minutes a day makes. (I know that sounds like a jingle from one of those horrible QVC infomercials, but it's true . . . and at least I'm not trying to sell you an over-priced tortilla warmer.)

Myth #6: Meditation is a spiritual or religious practice.

Enter Ed again, stage left. I often refer to meditation as centering when I use it with my coaching clients because the word is so often misunderstood. I can't tell you how often I've heard "C'mon, Shelley, if meditation isn't religious, then why do you sometimes see a Buddha or some sort of religious looking figurine on a meditation table?" And THAT is a very good question indeed.

The answer is that Buddhists don't actually pray to Buddha. To be honest, many Buddhists don't even believe in God. The Buddha figure is there as a reminder of the basic goodness we all share as human beings and a representation of the serenity and fulfillment we are capable of attaining through meditation. That's a long-winded way of saying it's an ideal to aspire to and emulate. That's it. And if you don't believe me, Google it.

Again, meditation is just focusing on the space between thoughts. I promise not to say it again.

Myth #7: I'm supposed to have transcendent experiences in meditation.

(Transcendent meaning surpassing the ordinary or exceptional.) In layman's terms, this would entail having visions, seeing bright colors, or even having that eerie out-of-body experience. Cue the theme from *The X-Files.* This sounds more like a close encounter of the third kind than a meditation session frankly. Beam me up, Scottie.

I've heard stories of these things occasionally happening during meditation and, if that's the case for you, then all I can say is enjoy the free high while it lasts. Don't get attached to it. Again, meditation is the practice of noticing space between thoughts. It's not about inducing a psychedelic state so you can zone out. If that's what you're really looking for, go to a Phish concert.

And now a few meditation myths of my own that are focused on what meditation is supposed to look and feel like.

Myth #8: You should feel calm, happy, and blissful when you meditate, otherwise something is wrong.

Think back to the quote at the beginning of this chapter. (There was a method to my madness.) In case you've forgotten it (I know, it's okay), here it is again:

> *"In meditation we discover our inherent restlessness. Sometimes we get up and leave. Sometimes we sit there, but our bodies wiggle and squirm, and our minds go far away. This can be so uncomfortable that we feel it's impossible to stay. Yet this feeling can teach us not just about ourselves but what it is to be human . . . we really don't want to stay with the nakedness of our present experience. It goes against the grain to stay present."*
> *~ Pema Chödrön*

The truth of the matter is meditation can often feel downright messy. Your mind is naturally going to want to yank you out of the present moment, to either the past or the future. That is how the mind works. It's very subtle and very sneaky but true. **If you're feeling resistance to meditating, then that is exactly why you should be meditating.** Our resistance to it demonstrates how much we actually need it. Take Pema's advice. She knows what she's talking about. Even though she's now a famous Buddhist monk, she used to be Deirdre Blomfield, grew up in New Jersey, has two kids, and was divorced twice. In other words, one of us.

Myth #9: Meditation has to be done with your eyes closed in silence sitting on a mat.

Meditation Quiz #2

Which of these could be meditative? (Circle all that apply.)

Running	Reading	Writing
Woodworking	Fishing	Yoga
Oil painting	Dancing	Stamp collecting

Okay, not stamp collecting. Really? Who does that anymore? All joking aside, the reality is that all of these things COULD be meditative for you. I find yoga helpful in calming the rushing river of thoughts, and I practice 4-5 times a week. That's the reason I often call it a moving meditation when I teach yoga to my students.

I've recently taken up oil painting and have been surprised at how meditative that is for me. The sessions last three hours and, during each one, my river of thoughts slows to a mere trickle. There is nothing else I can think of but the painting in front of me. It helps me achieve a level of focus that I never thought was possible. That is until my lovely art teacher snaps me out of the zone with a comment about how terrible my painting looks. We can't all be Picassos, can we?

Now, the idea of oil painting may make you want to run for the hills, and if so, you're not alone. The idea of fishing makes me feel the same way. But for SOME people, the rhythmic motion of casting the reel and recasting it, the sounds of the water lapping against the boat, and the pop of that tasty can of beer can make the experience highly meditative. All I can think about is having to put that dirty little worm on that big sharp hook, but hey, that's just me.

The trick is to figure out what slows the torrent of thought water for you. And if you think I'm taking too much license here, have no fear. Even Ed the monk would agree. There are many Buddhist-approved forms of meditation that are done with eyes completely open, even walking in a circle.

And last but not least . . . drumroll please!

Myth #10: People will think I'm a weirdo if I meditate.

I know this may sound silly, but for me that person was my husband. What will he think if he walks into my office and finds me meditating? Will he think I'm weird? Well, of course he thinks I'm weird. That's why he married me in the first place. In our relationship, I'm the equivalent of the spicy cheese to his bland macaroni. And another thing, what do I care what he thinks anyway? It's never stopped me before. And finally, what is he doing in my office anyway?

And after all that, the other day he was feeling really stressed at work and asked me how to meditate. In my infinite wisdom, I showed him.

Enough said.

Activity: Increase Your Meditation Moments

Like I keep saying, practice makes better. Take a moment to identify a couple of actions you can take to integrate meditation into your daily life. If you're not meditating currently, start small. Think about setting a goal for how often you meditate a week. What are the activities that slow down the thought flow for you? You may want to think about how you could increase these as part of your daily or weekly routine.

Action #1:

_____

_____

_____

_____

_____

Action #2:

_____

_____

_____

_____

_____

In summary:

- Meditation is the practice of focusing on the space between thoughts.

- Thoughts will come up when you're meditating. No biggie, skip the judgment, and bring your mind back to the present again and again.

- There are many different ways to mediate. There is no "correct" way.

- The benefits of meditation are heightened awareness, increased focus, greater emotional control, and stress reduction. Who wouldn't want that?

- There are a number of myths that hold us back from meditating. Don't be fooled.

- Start simple and be consistent.

In the next chapter, we're going to demystify the second most commonly misunderstood mindfulness practice, yoga. And don't be surprised to see Ed again. That mystical mindfulness monk gets a really good laugh out of what we Westerners have done with the practice.

Chapter 6

Yoga:

Why It's Better for You Than Yogurt

"The success of Yoga does not lie in the

ability to perform postures but in how it positively

changes the way we live our life and our relationships."

~ T.K.V. Desikachar

In this chapter:

- Definition(s) of Yoga

- Types of Yoga

- Shelley's Yoga Story

- Activity: Mind Body Connection

- Demystifying Yoga

- Tips for Starting a Yoga Practice

- Activity: Yoga Action Planning

I once asked a room full of corporate over-achievers to define the word yoga. The result, after a half hour of intense debate and scrutiny, was this:

An ancient method of relaxation designed to achieve inner

balance and harmony accomplished through performing a series of posture stretching exercises accompanied by regulated breathing and, in some instances, repeated chanting.

Yikes! Looks more to me like a literary train wreck achieved by over-complicating something simple to prove how smart you are. Just saying.

I was only looking for one word. One small, itty-bitty word. The word "union." And if you are wondering why, it's because that's what the word yoga literally means. (If they were really so dang smart, they would have just Googled it.)

Union of what you may ask? Well, that's simple too. Union of mind, body, and spirit. (Notice I said it was simple, not easy.) And if you think long and hard about what this actually means, it's really just code for mindfulness. The "holy trinity" of mindfulness to be precise, as each term refers to a different aspect of awareness – thought awareness (mind), physical awareness (body), and life purpose awareness (spirit, and hence why we spent so much time talking about this in the life intention chapter . . . there is a method to my madness). So, if you're in touch with all three of these, yay for you, as chances are you're living a pretty mindful life.

Now, as to how to go about doing it, this is where the yoga conversation tends to get deep and often esoteric because, as I'm sure you can imagine, there are many different views on how best to achieve that elusive union of mind, body and spirit. It all boils down to the immortal words of my straight-shooting grandmother. "There are many different ways to skin an armadillo" when it comes to yoga. (Remember, my family's from Texas.) Which explains why there are so many types of yoga: Hatha yoga (what Westerners typically associate as yoga, folks wearing tight outfits twisting themselves into pretzel-like formations while trying to maintain a peaceful zen-like feeling), Dhyana (what most folks would describe as sitting meditation . . . can you say ommmmmmm?), Karma yoga (the yoga of action and unselfishly doing good for others), Jnana yoga (the yoga of wisdom, e.g. is that chair real? – am I really here? – will the Texans ever make it to the Super Bowl? – will I ever finish this book?), and many more yogas.

For the purposes of this chapter, we're going to focus on hatha yoga for three reasons. First of all, it's more common than Starbucks, seeing as how you can't go more than ten feet before tripping over another new studio these days. Second, it's what most Westerners associate the word yoga with. And, finally, it's quite often misunderstood.

Now, back to the mind, body, spirit connection. Why on God's green earth would wearing a tight outfit and twisting yourself into a pretzel help bring about this elusive union? Good question, and it's one that I've asked myself a number of times throughout the years, because – make no mistake – hatha yoga does indeed have a very subtle and powerful way of bringing this transformation about. In order to enlighten you on how this can actually work, I'm going to share with you the story of my yoga journey. Hold on to your hat, it's a bumpy ride!

I'd like to say that what prompted me to start practicing yoga was the epiphany that I needed to make changes in my life – a sudden flash of inspiration brought on by careful self-reflection. Nope and nope. The real reason was much more noble. I was trying to impress this good-looking Scandinavian guy I was dating who brought me to my first yoga class. He was kind of a hippie and a do-gooder type, which was slightly annoying, but I figured I could put down my pack of cigarettes and glass of Chardonnay long enough to humor the poor fellow.

It was hot yoga. You may have heard of it – the kind that's done in a room heated to 105 degrees and at least 50% humidity. Think *Dante's Inferno* and the fiery levels of hell. Or if you didn't have the joy of being treated to a Catholic school education complete with delightful reading such as this, think about the Amazon rainforest. (I've never been, but I've heard it's a treat.) Hot, humid, and muggy, sweat dripping down your back the moment you step out of your lovely 5-star hotel. The air so thick with vapor you can barely breathe. Delightful.

We arrived at the studio. Jan (the guy, and it's pronounced Yawwwn, not Jan) sweetly paid for my class and put my mat down next to his. "What a keeper," I thought. Then class begins. I do my best to keep up with the postures despite this running dialogue in my head:

"*Oh my God, I look like a complete idiot. This outfit is way too tight. I look fat in my stomach. I really didn't think it was possible to sweat this much.*

Whoa! I'm starting to look like a drowned rat. My hair looks like a gigantic blonde afro! My makeup is running down my face.

Why is the teacher looking at me like that? She must think I'm stupid.

That student in front of me is laughing at me! Miss Priss . . . she thinks she's all that in her little pink Lululemon size zero outfit. Where the heck is my coccyx?

You want me to touch my forehead to my toes – wtf? Yeah, whatever Yoga Teacher Lady, not all of us are flexible like you and Miss Priss over there. She weighs about 90 pounds, of course it would be a piece of cake for her skinny ass. Bi#ch."

You get the picture. And this is the PG version.

"So what did you think of the class?" asks Jan.

"Great! Amazing! I've never done anything quite like it."

Three more classes and three weeks later, the bastard dumped me anyway.

But poor Jan had no idea the fire he had put a match to. I'd like to say that it was the realization that the yoga was doing me good that brought me back again and again, the sense that this practice was already starting to bring about that elusive union of mind, body and spirit. Nope and nope again.

I wanted to win. I was going to show this tree-hugging Scandinavian hippie who was boss. I was the better yogi (or was that yogini?) Whatever. Then I was going to take on Miss Priss too while I was at it. I didn't have an MBA and graduate at the top of my class for nothing. I thrive on competition. Bring it on!

And from these oh so noble intentions, my efforts started to bear fruit.

The Body

There is many a guru who has pontificated at some point that the body is really just a manifestation of what is going on in the mind. This idea played out for me in four very visible ways, which ultimately resulted in me boiling the frog, so to speak.

Ribbit. Boiling the frog? Okay, you've got a pot of water and a frog. Imagine what would happen if you dropped the frog straight into a pot of boiling water. It would probably jump out, right? I mean, the frog's not stupid after all. However, as the theory goes, if you put a frog in a pot of cold water and turn up the temperature gradually one degree at a time, it won't jump out. It will just sit there and happily hang out until the water temperature finally hits the danger zone. Then adios Mr. Frog. It's been nice knowing you.

So there I was in the pot of cold water, my mind gradually turning the temperature up and up, and just like Mr. Frog, I was completely oblivious to it all.

The first problem was my posture – which has never really been all that great despite the countless threats from my father that I was going to end up a hunchback. (Thanks, Dad, not quite Quasimodo yet.) I'm six foot one which, no matter how you slice it, is pretty tall for a woman. (Unless you live in the Netherlands or in some northern Scandinavian country where people say Ja! all day.)

While I am much more comfortable with my height now that I am an older and wiser adult who truly appreciates the advantages of being able to reach the top shelf in the kitchen without that rickety stool, this wasn't always the case. Imagine a tall, shy, eight-year-old girl with frizzy hair who was at least a foot taller than every other girl (and boy for that matter) in her class. A prize-winning recipe for insecurity if ever there was one. I learned pretty quickly that I needed to hide my height as much as possible to fit in, which, frankly, was a big waste of time because it never worked anyway. Over time, my shoulders sloped, and I developed a very pronounced slouch that was noticeable to everyone else but little old me. I was literally **wearing** my insecurity about my height.

Second, there was my weight, which was closely related to the posture problem because insecurities about my height and my outsider status prompted me to take comfort in food and poorly written romance novels. A bad cliché if ever I heard one. From about the age of eight until I started practicing yoga, my weight was a constant battle which fluctuated like a yo-yo throughout the years.

Third, over time my complexion started to take on a lovely hue of yellow due to the copious number of cigarettes I was smoking in my twenties and early thirties. Hey, I had an excuse. I had a stressful job after all. I worked in risk management in London. It was a dog eat dog world. Riding the tube in the morning was a full contact sport. My nerves were shot.

And last but most definitely not least, there was my hair. I'm sure you're familiar with the expression tearing your hair out, as in, "I've been tearing my hair out trying to get the job finished on time." Well, it's not just an expression.

At the age of sixteen, I was struggling with math. Keen as I was to get good grades, the thought of taking an algebra test would send me into a sheer panic. What if I fail? What if I don't know the answer? One day I looked down at the floor during math class, and there was a pile of hair lying there. That's interesting. Did some poor soul just lose a wig?

I looked around the room in a confused daze until I finally realized the hair was mine. Turns out it's a condition that even has a name, Trichotillomania (try saying it fast three times). I've often thought it sounds like the title of a bad horror movie or a Stephen King novel, but it really just means a person who pulls their hair out due to anxiety. Kudos to my hairstylists throughout the years for being as creative as you all were.

So how is it that a smart cookie like me didn't clue into the fact that these four things were having a profoundly negative impact on my life? In addition to the above, I was often sick, my drinking was increasing steadily, I was starting to feel more and more depressed, and, most importantly, where the heck was my Prince Charming? (He must have gotten stuck on the tube . . . damn Northern line.)

Again, think back to the frog in the pot. Ribbit. My water was getting hotter and hotter, but I wasn't noticing. After all, I had other more important things to do. I was in hot pursuit of the all mighty dollar (or in this case the all mighty pound). I was a mover and a shaker. I was the comptroller of an oil company in London by the tender age of 29. I had places to go, people to see. In other words, I was busy chasing the mechanical rabbit.

But that chase came with a steep price. I had become completely disconnected from my body and was treating it like it was some kind of disposable Pez dispenser. What I failed to grasp was how much my body impacted my mental state and vice versa. But before you picture me as some bald, yellow, hunchbacked creature from the black lagoon doomed for all eternity, there is hope!

So here's the funny thing about how yoga works. After I had been practicing it a few months, folks started commenting on how much better I looked. They mentioned a glow. That piqued my curiosity because I'd never been described as glowing, even when I was sweating like a pig during hot yoga class. Sure, I was losing weight. How could a person not in that fiery inferno of a studio? But it wasn't just my weight. I was standing up noticeably straighter, smoking less, and my hair was even getting a much-needed reprieve. And the most interesting part is that all of this was unconscious. Seriously. I mean, I didn't have to try. It just started happening. I kept doing yoga, and it kept happening.

High on this unexpected energy, I started trying crazy things like road bike riding and mountain climbing. Things I would have completely written off years before because I didn't have the balance, the coordination, the strength, the flexibility, or whatever excuse I was using for that particular week. After all, I had always been the smart one, not the sporty one. The sporty world was a world I didn't belong in. Hmmmm . . . could this be self-doubt? Sounds like yet another subtle and sneaky mindfulness block, don't you think?

Activity: Mind Body Connection

So enough about me. Now it's time to think about you.

1.   Where might your mind be having a negative impact on your body? Take just five minutes and write down whatever comes to mind.

_____

_____

_____

_____

_____

The Mind

"Shelley, it's interesting. You seem so calm at the moment. What is it you're doing differently?"

After the third time I heard this in one evening at a work cocktail party from three separate colleagues, I finally started to take notice. After all, three's a charm, right?

I was known in the department for doing good work, but come to find out I was also known for being highly strung. Since I had taken on the persona of being the smart, not sporty student early on in my adolescence, this followed me into adulthood. And the way these childhood stories manifest themselves is often very subtle and sneaky. I always had to have the answer. I mean, if I didn't, then that would mean I wasn't smart, right?

Now, as I'm sure you realize, unless you're Albert Einstein (which, even on a good day, I unfortunately am not), it's virtually impossible to have the right answer all of the time. And secondly, the esoteric yogini in me would now say, "What is right really after all?"

Given the nature of my past work, which included a lot of tight deadlines and highly pressurized situations, having the right answer all the time became more and more challenging as my responsibility and workload increased. Which, in turn, generated more and more panic, stress, confused thinking, and my other work nickname, Shelley The Chardonnay Queen. I mean, a girl's got to have an outlet for all that stress, right?

So back to the yoga. Unbeknownst to me, the yoga had inadvertently slowed down my flow of thought water. All those hours spent focusing on trying to hold myself in the shape of a pretzel were paying off in ways I could never have anticipated.

The Spirit

When I returned from my sabbatical where I learned how to teach yoga, I went back to my old life in risk management. It didn't last long. Clarity will often do that for a person. My body was cleaned up, my mind was cleaned up, and I now had no choice but to listen to my spirit, that quiet voice that had been there all along whispering in the background. That quiet voice that knew for so many years that I was living someone else's dream of what my life should look like.

As a life coach, I see this so often in clients. We all start off with great intentions and somehow along the way manage to get completely disconnected from the essence of who we are, our spirit. And it's not surprising. We're influenced by so many different people – parents, partners, friends, siblings, teachers, mentors, celebrities. They are very well intentioned and often have our best interests at heart. Many of them tell us what to do. Or maybe they don't, but we spend our time trying to please them anyway. And we do it because we want to belong. We do it unconsciously. And so we get lost.

Yoga taught me how to listen to my soul. And my soul was telling me it was time to make some serious changes and embrace who I really was. And so I did. And I've got to tell you, it's so much easier to live my version of my life than someone else's (plus the clothes fit much better too). I often wonder how my life would have ended up if Jan hadn't dragged me to that sweaty yoga studio on a Monday evening after work. I probably owe him a favor after all these years. Maybe I'll send him a free copy of this book. Maybe.

Demystifying Yoga

So, after reading that fabulous story of life-changing transformation, what's stopping you from jumping off that couch and heading to the first yoga studio you find? In keeping with the theme from the last chapter and given my tendency to make lists (the organized accountant in me still lives!), a good portion of this chapter is devoted to debunking the most common myths we tell ourselves about yoga that keep us from dusting off that ratty mat that lurks somewhere in the depths of our dark and musty closet.

Myth 1: I'm not flexible enough to do yoga.

Remember Miss Priss in her size zero Lululemon outfit? No matter how long I've been practicing and teaching yoga, I still fall into this trap from time to time. And it's hard not to when you look around and see some swan of a student in front of you who has absolutely no problem touching their head to their feet in a forward bend. I mean, really? I regularly tell my students that the reason I haven't gotten that far is my 36-inch inseam, and it's a long way down. It makes me feel better.

When a student tells me that a posture is just too difficult, there are two things I typically say – "Start where you are." and "Do what you can."

That's it. What were you expecting? Yoda?

So often we resist starting where we are. We view the practice as something that we need to get fit first in order to do. Or for those of us who are perfectionists (you know who you are), we view it as something that has to be done expertly, no margin for error allowed. Then we fill our minds with stories about why something is impossible, e.g. my legs are too long, I have a bad back, I'm not a flexible person. No matter what your physical condition is, there is always something you CAN do. No matter how small. Just the simple act of getting your body in motion is helpful.

This is also why many practitioners refer to yoga as a practice. It's a reminder that yoga is not about doing it perfectly. It's about practicing it. Each day you get up, do the best you can, and the next day you start all over again. And while this may sound a bit like *Groundhog Day*, it's also why we teachers often use the trite but true "It's about the journey, not the destination," when speaking about yoga.

Think back to the dog track yet again. So often we are so fixated on the rabbit that we forget to enjoy the ride. The ride is really the only thing that matters.

And here's the real clincher. Enter stage left Ed, The Mystical Mindfulness Monk.

Remember Ed?

According to Ed and his other mystical mindfulness monk friends, yoga really isn't about the postures at all. The yoga postures, or asanas as they are called, were invented for one reason – to focus your concentration. That's it. That's why I often call a hatha yoga class a moving meditation.

The postures are a tool for meditation and a tool for meditation only. They weren't invented for you to obsess over them and then constantly compare yourself to others in a cruel and self-depreciating way. That's just depressing.

So basically what that means is that, no matter what your posture looks like, as long as you are 100% concentrating on doing the posture, you are doing yoga. If your posture looks perfect, but your mind is working on creating a grocery list for when you hit the Shop and Save on your way home (some tasty cheese, some nice Chardonnay), you are not doing yoga. It's therefore not the what (the posture) but the how (how mindful you are when you're doing it) that's important when practicing yoga.

Sound familiar?

Myth 2: I need lots of special, expensive gear to do yoga.

You'd think so if you opened up a copy of *Yoga Journal* (yes, there is a magazine that is solely devoted to yoga). It's filled with many critical and life-changing questions like:

- Would a breathe mat help my yoga performance?
- Which Hydro Flask will keep my water at the optimum temperature?
- Which electrolyte mixture is best for keeping hydrated between classes?
- Should I try a onesie leotard or wear capris?

I don't care what you've read or who you have spoken to on this matter. You need two and only two things to do yoga. Yourself and a mat. That's it.

There are many folks who worry that, if they don't have the right outfit or right gear, they won't be doing it right. Don't be fooled. Yoga is a billion-dollar industry these days, and everyone is out to make a buck. Please don't misunderstand me. There's nothing wrong with buying a Hydro Flask if you really want one. The question I would ask you is why? Is it because optimum water temperature is really that important to you or because you want to fit in? We'd like to think that the older we get, the wiser we are, but often we're just as susceptible to falling into these traps as the five-year-old on the playground.

And it wouldn't be fair if I didn't share with you that I have fallen into many of these traps myself. And just for the record, a $90 leotard did not make me a better yogini. It just made me seriously irritated when I noticed the other day in class that the dye had already started fading. Namaste.

Myth 3: Yoga is for women.

Don't tell me you haven't thought it at least once, "Yoga's for chicks." Think this all you want, but I've noticed over the past few years of teaching yoga that the gender scales are becoming more and more balanced. In fact, I taught a class the other day that was almost entirely male. And don't be fooled my male readers, yoga is tough. There are a number of times when a sporty guy has walked up to me after his first class to tell me that it was one of the hardest things he's ever done. So, despite what you may think, it's not some pansy ass thing where you're sitting on a mat the entire time humming ommmmmmm in a pink leotard – although there are classes out there like that, and they are very beneficial in their own right.

And finally, if fame carries any weight with you, there are many sporting heroes that regularly practice yoga. At my old studio in Houston, the Texans (our professional football team that plays in the National Football League – just in case there's anyone in the world who doesn't know that, which I find very difficult to believe, but my editor told me to put this in) would regularly come in. Mind you, it still didn't get them into the playoffs . . . yet. Give it time, just give it time.

Shelley's Tips for Starting a Yoga Practice

But first, a fun Pop Quiz.

Which of the following are types of hatha yoga?

(Circle those that apply.)

Vinyasa	Hot yoga	Kundalini	Restorative
Ashtanga	Iyengar	Bikram	Yin

Yes, it was a little bit of a trick. (I couldn't help myself.) These are all forms of hatha yoga. Be aware, some studios nowadays even have another type specifically called hatha yoga (just to make things really complicated), but at the end of the day it's all just hatha yoga. Which leads me to the first tip for starting your yoga practice.

1. Try a few different styles.

Maybe you try a class, and it's too fast. Try another. Maybe you try one, and it's too slow. Try another. All of these different styles have their unique advantages. No style is better than another, despite what some studios will tell you. Most studios have introductory offers that are dirt cheap that last for a week or so where you have the opportunity to try a number of different classes. Make the most of it.

2. Go at least twice a week.

In order for the yoga to really be effective, you need to find a rhythm with it. If you're going sporadically, it's hard to get into the groove, so to speak. I recommend 2-3 times a week for a student who's just starting out. If you can do more than that, yay for you.

3. No expectations – just do your best!

Some classes you'll feel like you're completely in the zone, the stars are aligning, and you've got that posture nailed. Other classes you'll feel like crap. Literally. It happens no matter how long you've been practicing. The other day I got winded and had to sit down and take a break during one of the postures. Your body is different every day.

4. Try every posture.

Your mind will always come up with a million reasons why you can't do something if you let it. Your body is always stronger than you think it is. I have noticed in class that some students will often sit out a particular posture. They do this consistently every class. I know they can do it. I also know they really don't like to do it. I'm here to tell you that the posture that you hate the most is the posture that your body needs the most. Sorry, but that's just the way it works.

5. If you need to take a break, take one.

You're not Superman or Superwoman. Let go of the judgment. If you need to take a break during Downward Dog, take it. The only person that will be judging you is you. Everyone else is too busy trying to balance anyway.

Activity: Yoga Action Planning

Spend a few minutes identifying two actions you will take to progress your yoga practice. It could be taking a first step, such as identifying a studio in your area and signing up for your first class. If you're already practicing, it could be working on letting go of judgment or maintaining a consistent practice of 2-3 times a week.

Action #1:

_____

_____

_____

_____

_____

Action #2:

_____

_____

_____

_____

_____

In summary:

- Yoga is about union, in other words, bringing together the "holy trinity" of mindfulness: mind, body, spirit.
- There are many different types of yoga. Hatha yoga is the yoga of movement and what most westerners associate the word yoga with.
- Yoga works in subtle ways. Trust the process and just start practicing.
- Flexibility is not required to do yoga. Start where you are and do what you can.
- No expensive gear required. Just bring yourself, an open mind, and

a mat.

- Yoga is not just for chicks! It's increasingly becoming a gender-balanced practice.

- There are many different types of hatha yoga. Try a few different types when you start practicing.

- Let go of the judgment and don't compare your practice to others.

Now it's time to leave the ancient yoga world for more modern pastures. In the next to last (but certainly not least) chapter, we're going to take a long hard look at technology, including one of my favorite subjects – social media. Facebook, Twitter, LinkedIn, Pinterest – all wonderful inventions in their own right, but how are they impacting our ability to stay mindful?

Chapter 7

Technology and Mindfulness:

Is Being Wired Making Us Wired?

"We all need a technological detox; we need to throw away our phones and computers instead of using them as our pseudo-defense system for anything that comes our way. We need to be bored and not have anything to use to shield the boredom away from us. We need to be lonely and see what it is we really feel when we are. If we continue to distract ourselves so we never have to face the realities in front of us, when the time comes and you are faced with something bigger than what your phone, food, or friends can fix, you will be in big trouble."

~ *Evan Sutter, Solitude: How Doing Nothing Can Change the World*

In this chapter:

- Shelley's Top Technology Traps
- Shelley's Sad LinkedIn Story
- Shelley's Checklist for Safe Walking
- Activity: Your Technology Self-Assessment
- 18 Tips to Use Technology Mindfully
- Activity: Your Technology Action Plan

A few months ago I did the unthinkable. I deleted Facebook off my phone. I then proceeded to write a blog post about it that generated quite a bit of attention and discussion on social media. I have to admit I was surprised. Not that people liked my writing. I was surprised that so many folks adamantly asserted it was a positive thing to do.

How can this be? Aren't we all just chomping at the bit for the latest and greatest app or innovation that's going to revolutionize our lives? Interestingly enough, I guess not. And this got me thinking about mindfulness. (Which is a good thing considering it's the topic of this book.)

It also got me thinking about an experience many years ago, when I was a lowly financial analyst at ExxonMobil. I managed to get an invitation to an employee town hall the then CEO of ExxonMobil, Lee Raymond, was putting on. The big cheese was on a tour of the little island and wanted to meet with some of his worker bees. I was told I was selected on the basis that I was the extroverted American in the office and would be sure to ask an interesting question. Or at least a question. I don't think their criteria were super picky.

The day arrived, and I found the venue, which luckily was hard to miss given the crowd of angry Greenpeace protesters waving signs that said "Say no to Esso!" complete with pictures of Raymond with devil ears and a pitchfork (a particularly nice artistic touch I thought). I scrambled past the protesters and managed to get a seat in the front row.

I don't remember much of that talk. In fact, I don't remember any of it except for his response to one question, which I *didn't* ask by the way. He was asked why the company wasn't keeping up with the times when it came to social media, and this is how he responded. "There will come a time one day when real business and real relationships will matter again. And when it does, we'll be here."

Maybe that time is finally here.

When I think about the effect of technology on our lives, I can't help but think about my beloved dog track. With the help of technology, the dogs are now running faster and faster around that never ending track. The problem is the mechanical rabbit, now on supercharged batteries, is running faster too. So the chase continues, albeit at higher and higher speeds. And the result is that wonderful phenomenon we like to call burnout here in the west.

Now, this is not in any way to say that technology is bad. That would be judgment, and as you may recall, judgment is not super helpful when it comes to mindfulness. When it comes to technology, it's not so much the what as it is the how. Sound familiar?

What I mean by this statement is that a large portion of how we consume technology is unconscious. And if you think I'm wrong, I dare you to download one of those apps that will monitor how many times a day you check your phone. You'll be floored. Even myself, the Irreverent

Guru of Mindfulness that I am, was shocked when I looked at my statistics for the first time.

And it's not limited to phones. The next time you grab that TV remote, think about this. To what extent are you consciously watching what's there? Or are you mindlessly flipping through the channels while at the same time thinking about your to do list?

As a former smoker this all makes perfect sense to me. There is a new addiction that is sweeping the world. No country, gender, or ethnicity is left unscathed. I've been out to the far-reaching corners of Africa, and it's everywhere. Even the Maasai tribesmen in Kenya, who not that long ago thought their soul would be stolen if someone took their picture, had cell phones. I mean, who wouldn't want a selfie after you've speared that lion? Selfies over souls any day of the week.

So having said all that, it's probably worth taking a look at exactly how technology is impacting mindfulness. And in order to do so, I've taken the liberty of creating yet another fun and exciting list, entitled Shelley's Top Technology Traps. (It's got a nice ring to it, doesn't it?)

Trap #1: 24 hours a day, 365 days a year, I am here . . .

You get up in the middle of the night for a much needed glass of water and look down at your phone, which just so happens to be lying on the nightstand next to your bed. You see an urgent email from a client in a different time zone that's six hours ahead. Dang it! Now you're up the rest of the night for one of two reasons. One – you're now at your computer working on a response. Two – you're back in bed, vainly trying to sleep while all the time worrying about the email and how you're going to make time to address it in your already overstuffed day. Either way, you end up at work the next morning tired and in a cranky mood. "What's got into her this morning?" a colleague wants to know.

Or maybe you were smart enough to turn your phone off for the night. It still doesn't change the fact that these days everyone expects a response right away. Did you get that email I sent you? Did you get my text?

The problem this poses from a mindfulness perspective is one of space. Think back to meditation. It works because it gives a person a chance to see and experience the space between their thoughts. From that space comes peace. From that space comes inspiration.

Think about it. How many times have you gone to bed with something weighing on your mind to wake up the next morning and have the answer? Or you go for a walk and come back to your computer and suddenly – voilà – you have the solution to the problem you were grappling with? This isn't a coincidence. It's the magic of space. Humans need space. It's almost as important as food, water, and that next episode of *The Real Housewives*.

The second problem this poses from a mindfulness perspective is more subtle. With all that time responding to everyone else's email and text messages, when is there time for you? Your vision? Your goals? Your life intention? As a coach, I see it all the time. Folks tell me that they need more "work/life balance." They're dragged in a million directions at once. They never have any time for themselves. They feel like they're on a treadmill and can't get off. It always makes me think of one of those hamsters stuck in that wheel thing. Did you ever have one of those as a kid? It can be said a thousand different ways but these comments are normally code for, "I need to get my priorities straight."

The more you allow yourself to get dragged away from your life intention, the less energy you'll have and the more put out you will feel. It's just a fact. We have energy for what's most important to us. One of my favorite quotes is one I have creatively paraphrased from Stephen R. Covey (who knew a thing or two about personal effectiveness). If you know what's important to you, when you say no, you're really saying yes to something much bigger.

Trap #2: FOMO or, in other words, Fear of Missing Out

I was playing around on my computer the other day and Googled this one. To my surprise there was a definition that popped straight up:

"FO•MO

fōmō

noun

informal

Anxiety that an exciting or interesting event may currently be happening elsewhere, often aroused by posts seen on a social media website.

Example: I realized I was a lifelong sufferer of FOMO."

A lifelong sufferer of FOMO? OMG! WTF! SIIS! (You don't know SIIS? "Say it isn't so." Okay, I just made that one up.)

It's the proverbial grass is greener complex which has only gone into overdrive with the advent of social media. If you have kids, you're no stranger to this one. "Susie's at Disney World, I want to go to Disney World too!" And that fun day at the park that you were doing your best to orchestrate at that moment in time is no match for Mickey Mouse.

But before you shake your finger at your kids in disgust, look in the mirror. Think about the last time you've been stuck at some event where you really didn't want to be. Perhaps it was Aunt Ingrid's 85th birthday party down at Shady Acres Retirement Home. Don't tell me that you weren't checking your phone, looking around for something better to do, and felt a pang of anguish when you spied one of your friends lounging on the beach in St. Kitts. They may have the beach, but remember, that applesauce at Shady Acres is hard to beat.

The most interesting example of the grass is always greener I've heard of in a while was from one of my single girlfriends. She accepted a date with a guy she had met online. On paper, this guy looked like Mr. Right, so she got all dolled up in her glam rags and made sure she arrived on time.

Amazingly enough, he did even look like his picture. Things were off to a smashing start. During the date she noticed Mr. Right kept looking down at his phone and sending texts. Hmmm . . . maybe his mother was sick? Some sort of emergency for sure. When she finally questioned him on this, he mentioned that he was checking in with dates #2 and #3 for the evening. Evidently her slot as date #1 was almost up. To make a long story short, I don't believe she saw him again.

Trap #3: If it's not on Facebook, it didn't happen.

Or Instagram, or Twitter, or Snapchat, or the like. Pick your poison. And so we go to great lengths to document the moment for prosperity. Maybe we even go the whole hog and buy a selfie stick.

I'll never forget the first time I actually saw one of these. I happened to be in San Francisco with my best friend Lena. We were happily strolling down the seafront and decided to visit the sea lions at Pier 39. As we approached the pier, we saw a group of giggly young girls using these contraptions. We were entranced, we couldn't look away. They spent countless minutes not looking at the lions, but vying for that perfect selfie shot. Maybe they finally saw the lions when they posted the photo to Instagram.

The other day I happened to get a free pass to the highly popular South by Southwest (SXSW) music festival held annually here in Austin. (If you happen to be a hipster, you'll know it instead by its abbreviated name "South by.") Being the thrifty person that I am, I took advantage of the opportunity and showed up at a local bar to listen to some music. Cheap is good, but free is better I always say. I stayed for a couple of acts and watched the other spectators. (I must admit I used it as an opportunity to do a little research.) Half of the audience was busy recording the experience via picture or video. The other half was busy on their smartphones, checking out the next show. Maybe the latter half had been afflicted by FOMO too?

Trap #4: Please like my photo, please???

Starting a business is humbling where yours truly is concerned, especially when you're initially gearing up. I went to all this trouble to create these wonderful blog posts full of entertaining and highly amusing mindfulness moments, and no one even freaking bothered to look. And that's when I started this:

"Are you kidding me? I wonder what this means. Why didn't Carol respond? That bit#h.

She's probably just jealous of me. I think she's always been secretly jealous of me. I know she's always wanted to quit her day job and start a business. Maybe I'll unfriend her. I never liked her all that much anyway.

And while I'm at it, I'll unfriend Jack too. I mean, what has he ever done for me?

Or maybe no one really likes me. Maybe this means I'm going to be a failure. No one is ever going to read this book. No one is ever going to listen to my podcasts. I bet no one will even register for my mindfulness course at UT. I'm going to end up penniless and broke on the streets of Austin, holding up one of those cardboard signs.

What was I thinking? I must be some sort of hack. Irreverent Mindfulness Guru no way. I'm not even fit to clean the boots of mindfulness masters like Deepak Chopra or Jon Kabat-Zin. Maybe I should stop all this compulsive worrying – Hey! Isn't worrying a mindfulness block by the way? – and get back to what I was doing. What was I doing??? Oh yeah, writing this

book."

Trap #5: My smartphone, my BFF.

I was intrigued by a series of photos that an American photographer put together recently. He asked subjects to pose with their mobile phones as part of their normal daily routine and then took away the phone. The result was something like this:

I mean, who needs a partner when you can have a smartphone? Perhaps at some point we'll trade the real thing for virtual sex. It's probably less messy that way.

Forget personal relationships for a second. Imagine that you're giving a presentation on your latest project at work. You've psyched yourself up, spent hours and hours preparing. It's finally your big moment. Halfway through your slide on the amazing new marketing strategy you're about to launch, you look out at your audience and notice that about half of them are staring at their smartphones. How does that make you feel? I realize I'm not a therapist, but this is important to think about. If you happen to be in the audience, what message are you sending? Communication isn't just what we say; it's also what we do. It's how we show up in the moment.

I used to teach a course on influence. A large part of the second day was devoted to listening. Listening, really? That's so old school! So nineties. Surely influence is more about crafting a well-constructed argument with the latest and greatest leadership development techniques than listening. Nope, it's really not. Surveys say the most influential people in our lives tend to be the ones who really listen to us. Hard to do when you're also checking your email on your smartphone.

Trap #6: Huh? Sorry, I just need to send this email quickly.

The other day I wrote a blog post (which luckily a few people did manage to read) that was all about the perils of multitasking. It was focused on a day that started out innocently enough. A colleague sent me an email to register for a new free referral database so we could trade referrals. Good idea I thought, and clicked on the link. I filled in my info and set up an account. Easy peasy. Then I saw a notice for a way to easily add contacts to the referral system through uploading a LinkedIn file. It looked simple enough.

It was right before lunch, and I had an appointment to get to, and time was running short. My thoughts were occupied with the lunch meeting, what I was going to say to my potential client, which route I would take to get to the restaurant, what I would order when I got there. I also had a number of things open on my desktop, emails that needed sending, tasks that still needed to be completed.

Before I even realized what I had done, I saw a screen pop up that said "Invitation sent to 756 contacts." Ummmmm, say what? And then the realization. I had just inadvertently emailed my entire LinkedIn contact list – every single person that I'm connected to – with something that may only be relevant to about 50 of them.

What happened next was that horrible sinking feeling – you know – the one you get when you start to panic. The one that's normally accompanied by thoughts of, "My God, I really am the biggest doofus ever!" or "I'm an evil spammer who's no better than a sleazy used car salesman!"

These thoughts occupied me as I ran down my stairs in a haze, late for my lunch meeting now. I heard a very loud yelp as I hit the bottom of the staircase. In my haze, I had failed to notice my cat Bijoux lying on the stairs and had inadvertently stepped on her paw. After one emergency trip to the vet and $150 later, Bijoux is now fine I'm glad to report.

And the moral to this story you may ask? Concentration DOES matter, even when you're doing menial tasks. "Well, I only really multitask when I'm doing admin-like stuff that doesn't matter all that much."

That's what I thought. You and I may want to rethink that.

Trap #7: I SO can Google and drive my car at the same time.

Ummmmm, no you can't. I know you really, really think that YOU can, but you can't. For some reason, we fool ourselves into thinking that we are exempt from this rule. It's all those other drivers out there that can't drive. You know, the ones that don't know how to use their blinkers and drive too slow in the fast lane.

Forget driving though. Walking is now becoming increasingly dangerous in the technology age. Why you ask? Because we are too busy looking at our smartphones to look up. I was recently on the SXSW homepage, gearing up for my day of free music and revelry, when I noticed a checklist of do's and don'ts. Safe walking is so much a concern now to the organizers of the event that it even warrants a checklist. Here's mine:

Step 1: Put phone away.

Step 2: Put one foot in front of the other.

Step 3: Go.

Trap #8: Having a crick in my neck is the new cool thing.

Now this is not to say that technology doesn't have its merits when it comes to health. Back when I was still in the corporate world, I had one of those company-issued Fit Bits. And I will say that it did drive many of us to become much more conscious of our activity levels. "Come on, Aimee, let's walk to the coffee bar to get some peanut butter cups. We'll get steps."

I did hear about some unscrupulous company employees who attached theirs to their dogs however. All I can say to you people is cheaters never win. (Okay, I'll admit it. I kind of wish I'd thought of it first.)

As a yoga teacher, I'm hearing people complain more and more about pain in the upper part of their necks from looking down so much at their hand-held technology. The other day, I came across a very amusing video on YouTube. I stopped laughing once I realized it was an actual news report from China. Evidently the problem is so bad there that teenagers are having their heads put in slings as a way of correcting the damage frequent phone and tablet use is doing to their postures.

In addition to these physical pains, there's no shortage of mental ones. More and more studies are coming out that show that frequent usage of social media is linked to depression. And it's not surprising considering the fact that there is always going to be some soul out there that has a better life than you – at least so it seems on the surface. A happier life, a more stress-free life, a more successful business, a better-looking

161

boyfriend or girlfriend, a nicer house, or however you define success. It's all great fodder for the dogs at the track that are still trying to chase that mechanical rabbit. You'd think they'd have learned by now, wouldn't you?

Okay, enough about the problem. So what's the solution? Before you throw that smartphone out the window of a moving car, there is hope. Remember, I said earlier it's not the what, but the how that's important when it comes to technology. Am I consciously choosing to do this because it will serve a purpose? Or am I doing this unconsciously or out of habit? When thinking about my own usage, I often find it helpful to ponder the following:

- What is my relationship to technology and social media? How does it define me?
- How does it affect me – both negatively and positively?
- How does it affect my relationships – both negatively and positively?
- How conscious am I when using it?

Activity: Your Technology Self-Assessment

And since there is no time like the present (did you get the mindfulness reference?), get cracking! Spend the next ten minutes answering each of the following questions:

1. What is my relationship to technology and social media? How does it define me? (Think about your motivations for using it, particularly when

it comes to social media.)

_____

_____

_____

_____

_____

2. How does it affect me – both negatively and positively? (Think back to the Top Technology Traps. Which ones resonated most with you? What impact may these be having on your ability to focus, listen, innovate, think clearly, or even manage stress?)

_____

_____

_____

_____

3. How does it affect my relationships – both negatively and positively? (Think about both personal and work relationships for this one.)

_____

_____

_____

_____

4. How conscious am I when using it? (You may want to run through an entire day in your mind when thinking about this one. When is the first time you use technology in the morning? E.g. are you grabbing the phone first thing before you even say good morning to your precious hubby? When is the last time you use it in the evening?)

_____

_____

_____

_____

_____

You may find that this activity revealed some places where change could be a little helpful. Let's spend some time now thinking about what that could look like. When I'm facilitating mindfulness programs this is a question I often ask. On the next page, is a small selection of what I've heard – helpfully labeled and numbered for your reference!

<u>18 Tips to Use Technology Mindfully</u>

1. Place your phone out of reach when you're driving in the car. If you can't reach it, you won't be tempted to check it.

2. Create smartphone ground rules for business meetings. Pass around a basket at the beginning of meetings to collect phones.

3. Delete apps like Facebook off your phone. Don't worry. It will still be on your computer.

4. Only check social media during a set period of time each day.

5. Install an app like Checky on your smartphone that tells you how often you're checking your phone each day.

6. Make your bedroom a technology-free zone. Remove the TV. Seriously.

7. Stop using your smartphone as an alarm. Turn it off during the night. Get an alarm clock instead.

8. Stop viewing your phone first thing in the morning.

9. Turn work email off on your phone when leaving work.

10. Create ground rules at home for phone usage, e.g. no phones at the dinner table.

11. Eliminate distracting apps from your phone.

12. Utilize mindfulness apps on your phone. There is one I utilize called 7s Meditation. Each day I get a message that reminds me to practice mindfulness.

13. Call the person instead of always defaulting to text or email.

14. Install a gratitude app as a way of doing some daily personal reflection.

15. When on a work conference call, close your email and any other applications that are currently open. Practice deep listening.

16. Turn email notifications off on your work computer. They dilute your focus. Get into the habit of only checking work email at certain times of day.

17. Take periodic breaks throughout the day to walk around the office. Outdoors is best.

18. Make sure your workstation is set up ergonomically.

Couldn't have said it better myself. And you'll notice that none of these include chucking your smartphone out the car window. I'd also like to point out that many of these suggestions describe ways to utilize technology for the better. Again, it's not the what but the how.

Activity: Your Technology Action Plan

So, now it's time for you to put it into practice. Spend a few minutes writing down a couple of actions you'd like to start right away.

Action #1:

_____

_____

_____

_____

_____

Action #2:

_____

_____

_____

_____

_____

In summary

- Technology isn't right or wrong, good or bad when it comes to mindfulness. The question is how you're using it. Am I consciously choosing to do this because it will serve a purpose? Or am I doing this unconsciously or out of habit?

- Beware of the Top Technology Traps. Technology, if used wisely, can increase mindfulness. If used unconsciously and carelessly, it can often exacerbate mindlessness.

- Periodically ask yourself a series of questions to analyze how you're using technology, and if you need to make changes, make them.

  - What is my relationship to technology and social media? How does it define me?

  - How does it affect me – both negatively and positively?

  - How does it affect my relationships – both negatively and positively?

  - How conscious am I when using it?

- There are a number of steps you can take to increase the mindfulness of your technology usage. The key is to make your usage as intentional and conscious as possible.

Well, folks, that was the last piece that needed to fall into place in the proverbial puzzle. Now that we've solved the technology problem, it's time to finally bring it all together so that you can confidently take these concepts out into the world to impress your friends, family, and colleagues as the mighty mindfulness guru you now are.

In the next and final chapter, join me for The Adventures of Mindless Mona. As you will soon see, poor Mona has a very bad day. A day that could very much have been avoided if only dear Mona had been as smart as you were when you picked up this book and read it. In fact, I think I'll send her a free copy, the generous Irreverent Guru of Mindfulness that I am.

Chapter 8

The Adventures of Mindless Mona:

The Perils of a Mindless Day

"Running on empty

Running on, running blind

Running on, running into the sun

But I'm running behind.

Gotta do what you can just to keep your love alive

Trying not to confuse it with what you do to survive

In sixty-nine I was twenty-one and I called the road my own

I don't know when that road turned into the road I'm on."

~ *Jackson Browne, Running on Empty*

I've been told over the years that I have a knack for making things practical. Relatable. Accessible. And as thankful as I am for this innate ability, it doesn't sound as glamorous as having a knack for song, poetry, or even dance. I'm flashing back to a memory of a twelve-year-old me with a microphone attempting to belt out a heartfelt rendition of *Wind Beneath*

Your Wings. You know, no matter what Langston Hughes wrote, some dreams really are just better left deferred. But I digress. Back to my knack.

So in the spirit of real world application and all things practical, this final chapter is devoted to the story of Mindless Mona. The hapless victim of a day filled with extreme mindlessness. A poor dear soul who falls prey to the perils of living on autopilot. A relatable reminder of why this topic is just so darn important. A fitting finale for this epic journey into mindfulness. And besides, who doesn't love a good tall tale, right?

And who better to share this adventure with me than Ed, The Mystical Mindfulness Monk?

+++

"Okay, I've got the popcorn. Did you bring the Cheetos?"

"What Cheetos?" asks Ed.

"The Cheetos I told you to bring. I can't watch a movie without Cheetos."

"You didn't say anything about Cheetos."

"Yes, I did." (I have to admit I'm just a tad cheesed off at Ed right now.)

"No, you didn't."

"Okay, you're starting to piss me off, Ed! We need to get started. Time is money."

"Tell me again what we're watching, Shelley?"

"Jesus, Ed! Don't you ever listen? The Adventures of Mindless Mona. An engaging, witty, and downright thought-provoking story I made up to illustrate the dangers of living mindlessly. Plus it illustrates how to apply the tips in this book to your day-to-day life. Pretty clever of me, right?" (Okay, I admit I may be just the teeniest bit desperate for Ed's approval.)

"I'll be the judge of that," Ed replies.

"Everyone's a critic. Just hit Play, will you?"

+++

Beep, beep, beep, beep!

Mona groans as she gropes for her phone and hits the snooze button. She rolls over in bed and buries her head under the pillow.

She's exhausted.

And well she should be.

She's tossed and turned since two a.m. That fateful hour when she woke up to use the bathroom and just happened to glance down at her phone that's oh so conveniently located on her bedside table.

And there it was, in red caps to boot. "URGENT: PROBLEM WITH THE WRIGHT ACCOUNT"

"Did she really need to use all caps?"

The email was from her boss of course, whom Mona not so affectionately refers to as Wendy, the Workaholic Witch.

"Damn it! Doesn't she have a life? Who sends an email like that
at eleven at night? This account is going to be the death of me!
It's been nothing but trouble from day one. I never should have
let Wendy talk me into making that proposal. There are some
clients you just don't need at the end of the day."

And this was how Dear Mona started her Wednesday. Oh so positive and poised for success!

++

"Ed! Put your phone down!"

"Hey! I'm not bothering anyone. It's on silent."

"I don't care. You're supposed to be paying attention. You're supposed to be watching the movie with me." (I'm a stickler for process.)

"I was paying attention. So she tossed and turned all night. Poor Mona.

So what?"

"Didn't you read Chapter 7, or were you too busy playing Tetris on your phone?"

"Don't knock Tetris, Shelley. It's a great mindfulness practice. Plus it helps with my spatial skills."

"Tetris as a mindfulness practice? Give me a break, Ed! So you noticed that Mona hasn't set proper smartphone boundaries, right? If she hadn't checked the phone in the middle of the night, this never would have happened." (I'm trying not to sound judgmental, because that wouldn't be very mindful of me, would it?)

"But the email would still be there in the morning," Ed points out.

"Yes, the email would still be there. But at least she'd be dealing with it after she'd had a full night's sleep and was well rested."

"Okay, point taken, Shelley. But look, all Mona needs to do is sit down in a quiet place and spend the next hour or so meditating. She'll feel much better then."

"Are you crazy, Ed? She's already overslept and needs to get to work. Not everyone has the luxury of being able to zone out on a mat all day long like a certain monk I could name but won't. Hit Play again."

++

Scrambling to get dressed, Mona looks down at her watch, knowing that she'll be late for work for sure at this rate.

"Great. And I bet Wendy will be there waiting to pounce on me, like some nasty spider, as soon as I walk in. No time for breakfast today. One of those frozen Eggo waffles will work just fine. Wow! Bill's right. This thing really does taste like cardboard."

And, with Wendy on her mind, Mona narrowly misses bumping into her husband Bill as she comes flying out of the kitchen.

"Hey, Babe! You look really worn out."

"Thanks, you're too kind." She wasn't too tired for sarcasm.

"I'm just concerned, Mona. I'm not sure you're getting enough sleep. What about using that meditation app before you go to sleep? You know, the one Janet mentioned the other day when she and George were over for dinner."

"I'll think about it," Mona replies with an insincere smile.

"Yeah right. Janet is such a know-it-all."

"So I'll see you at the restaurant at 6:30 tonight, right, Babe?"

"Was that tonight?"

"Yeah. Okay. Sounds great, Bill."

"Remember, it's at the new location this year."

"Yep," replies Mona, her head halfway inside her purse as she rummages around.

"Where the hell are my damn car keys?"

+++

"See? It's like I said. Meditation. Even her husband thinks she should be meditating! Although I'm not a big fan of those meditation apps. Better if she would just develop the discipline to do it on her own," Ed remarks somewhat smugly.

"Oh please, who died and made you Mr. Meditation?"

"I'm a monk. It's what I do."

"We all just start where we are, Ed. There's nothing wrong with those meditation apps. After all, we're striving for excellence, not perfection. Now, that frozen Eggo waffle on the other hand . . ."

"This from the woman who wanted me to bring a jumbo-sized bag of Cheetos?"

"So you did remember, Ed! You just chose not to comply."

"You shouldn't be eating that junk anyway, Shelley. You'll thank me later."

"You sound just like my mother."

"Do I? I'm sure she's a very sensible woman."

"Hit Play, Ed."

+++

"Okay, so when I walk in, I'll take the back door near the coffee machine, grab a quick cup, and make my way around to my desk. If I can just get to that Wright account email first,

175

hopefully I'll be able to put out the fire before the meeting on the Brown & Company proposal.

Crap! I just missed my exit! Crap, crap, crap!

It's okay, Mona. Just turn around. Turn around. No biggie.

Okay, here we go . . . wait a second . . . Since when have they been doing construction here? Jeez, what a mess! Maybe I can take a shortcut through this neighborhood."

One speeding ticket in a school zone later, and Dear Mona is approaching the parking garage.

"I can't believe that cop! I couldn't have been going as fast as he said.

Okay, parking garage ahead, finally here.

Where the heck's my keycard? I could have sworn I put it in my purse yesterday after work. Crap! It's not here!

Crap, crap, crap!

Okay, no biggie, Mona. Just push the button for the security guard.

Answer for God's sake! Why aren't you answering?! Off on another doughnut break, Barney?"

Honk! Honk!

Mona turns and looks behind her.

"Oh my God! I can't believe how rude some people are!"

"Just wait a second, please!" Mona yells out the car window. "I can't find my keycard, and the security guard isn't answering!"

Honk! Honk!

"I can't believe how obnoxious this so-and-so is being!

Whatever happened to common decency? Chivalry?"

Mona looks down at her watch again as she races to the elevator. Forty-five minutes late. Not too bad all things considered.

++

"That guy in the parking garage was a real jerk," remarks Ed.

"That's your opinion. Or maybe he was in a hurry too and had something else on his mind. Did you ever think of that?"

"Oh, c'mon! You would have gotten pissed off too, Shelley, especially at the lazy parking attendant. Where was he by the way?"

"Someone's a little high on judgment this afternoon, isn't he?" (I love it when Ed isn't Mr. Perfect Mystical Mindfulness Monk.)

"I call it like I see it."

"Would you still call him lazy if he had rushed off to help someone in an emergency, Ed? Besides, if Mona hadn't been in such a rush and forgotten her keycard in the first place, this never would have happened." (I mean, facts are facts, right?)

"Fair enough, Shelley, but I'm really starting to feel sorry for Mona. She's really getting dumped on."

"You're emotionally connecting with the character. I'll take that to mean that you're finding my story highly believable and very engaging."

"Just hit Play, would you?" grumbles Ed.

+++

"Okay, so if I can just get to my desk without Wendy noticing, all will be well. The coast is clear. Excellent, now I've got my cup of coffee.

Now if only that person would get out of my way! Move it, Buster!"

"Excuse me. Excuse me. Sorry," Mona mutters as she passes the last roadblock standing between her and her desk.

She collapses into her chair and breathes a sigh of relief. Luckily, Wendy is nowhere to be seen.

Mona looks at her messy desk. The birthday plant from her well-intentioned colleagues is now a nice shade of brown.

"I should probably throw that away."

"Hi, Mona! Too busy to say hi to me?"

She looks up from the dying plant.

"What's got you in such a rush?"

"Oh my God! The division head, Ameet! That's right. Wendy told me he was going to be in town today from Chicago. You can forget about making that good impression now, Mona!"

"Ameet, hi! Sorry! I didn't see you there."

And as Mona jumps up to shake Ameet's hand, her arm bumps her coffee cup, and its contents go flying all over her new dress.

"Ouch! Damn it! That coffee's hot! Oh, great impression, Mona,

you moron. Way to go. Now he thinks you're rude and clumsy."

One trip to the bathroom, where she notices her earrings are mismatched, and two emergency KitKats later, it's time for the Brown & Company meeting.

+++

"You don't think the coffee was a bit much, Shelley? She could have scalded herself!"

"Just pretend it was lukewarm."

"You know, I could really go for a KitKat right now."

"Ed, concentrate! No mindless eating. You're turning into Mona. Okay, what did you notice about that scene?" I ask in my best mindfulness schoolmarm tone of voice.

"Well Mona obviously made a fool of herself in front of the big cheese. She was thinking so much about what was the next thing to do that she couldn't see what was right in front of her."

"Fool implies judgment, Ed, just in case you were wondering. But you're right about Mona being caught up in the next thing to do. Her mind was definitely a million miles away."

179

"What's wrong with a little judgment?"

"Didn't you read Chapter 3, Ed?"

"Maybe. What was it about again?"

"Judgment, you nit!"

"Hey! Who's being judgmental now? Take a few deep breaths, Shelley. I'll loan you my prayer beads if you want."

"Just hit Play," I spit out through clenched teeth.

++

"Oh God, Ameet is going to sit in on this meeting. Better not say anything stupid. Hopefully the stain on my dress isn't that noticeable. I can't believe it – I just bought this thing! Okay, nothing you can do about it now. Put on your cheery voice."

"Hi there, guys!" Mona says a little too brightly.

"Hey there," the rest of her team mutters without looking up from their smartphones.

"Good morning, Mona. Did you get that email I sent you last night?"

"Sure thing, Wendy. First priority, right after this meeting."

"Great. It's really important you get on that today. I want to have a response ready by close of business."

"Sure thing, Wendy. I'll get right on it."

"A response today? Is she kidding?! I'm going to have to do a lot of research to solve this problem. I'm not a miracle worker!

180

How am I supposed to get all this done?"

Suddenly she feels that familiar pain in her stomach.

"Did I remember to take my blood pressure medication this morning? I don't think I did. I really need to be more consistent about that. My doctor isn't going to be happy with me.

It's all this mess with the Wright account. If only that account would just go away.

Let's see. If I can get the cost projections from Finance today, I may be able to get an answer to that email. I need to see if I can sweet talk Jamie into doing that for me. He likes me.

I helped him on that thing from Mark the other day. Quid pro quo.

Is Kerry looking at the stain on my dress?"

Mona shifts uncomfortably in her chair to hide the stain.

"Did you get that, Mona?" asks Wendy.

"Yep."

"Get what?"

Mona looks around the room, an unconvincing smile on her face.

"Great, because you're going to be taking the lead on this proposal so it's really key you understand all the ins and outs."

"Sure thing, Wendy."

"Oh crap. What the hell is she talking about? Crap, crap, crap!

Okay, no biggie, just pay attention now."

But try as she might, Mona's thoughts keep wandering back to the Wright account.

"It's all my fault. I should have set clearer expectations about customer service up front. I'm always doing this. Over-promising and under-delivering. When am I going to learn?"

The meeting finally over, Mona rushes back to her desk to get to work on the Wright account.

++

"No, it's not your fault, Mona! Wendy's working you too hard!"

"Get a grip, Ed."

"Could you just throw her a bone, Shelley? At least heal the high blood pressure, for heaven's sake?"

"Maybe. I'll think about it."

"Mona's so hard on herself," Ed says in a worried tone of voice. "It's got her all over the place. She can't concentrate. Her mind is so jumbled up now with self-doubt and criticism that she's missing everything that's going on in that meeting."

"Yep, good old self-doubt. Sounds like a sneaky mindfulness block to me. Remember Chapter 4, Ed? Now Mona's all caught up in her story about how she never gets it right. The longer that sad old tune plays in her head, the less present she is. When it comes right down to it, we're our own worst critic," I conclude.

"She needs to start practicing that self-compassion stuff you talk about."

"Ah ha! So you did read Chapter 3 after all!" I exclaim triumphantly.

"Just the good parts. Hit Play."

+++

"Okay, concentrate. Let's get this Wright thing done."

Mona looks up at the sound of the ding and sees a new email in her inbox. The subject line grabs her attention.

"Those idiots in Procurement! They never get anything right!

I sent her the details for that PO over a week ago."

And she fires off an angry response.

But what Dear Mona doesn't know is the carefully crafted email she supposedly sent over a week ago to Procurement is still sitting in her drafts folder, ready to send.

Oops.

+++

"Ugggh. She's really going to regret that later," Ed says, shaking his head sadly back and forth.

"Yep."

"I'm sure she didn't mean to do it. She's just having a bad day. If she'd just stayed curious and not jumped to conclusions. If she'd just asked a few more questions, she might have realized the email is still in her drafts folder."

"Quite possibly. A curious mind is a mindful mind. But we'll never know. It's too late now."

"Rewrite it, Shelley!"

"No."

"C'mon!"

"No!"

"You're a hard woman, Shelley. A hard woman."

"This isn't called the Adventures of *Mindful* Mona. If she did everything right, this story would be boring. If she had simply disabled the email notification, she probably wouldn't have responded right there and then in an agitated state. A smart mindfulness practitioner would only check their email a couple times a day to eliminate distractions."

"Oh would they, Miss Smarty Pants?"

"Yes, they would, and you know it. Now be a good little mystical mindfulness monk and hit Play."

+++

"I don't know why they ever hired her. It must have been a favor. I heard her parents know Ameet. Childhood friends or something."

"What's going on?" asks Mona, as she grabs another cup of coffee and a doughnut from the breakroom.

"Just one doughnut won't hurt."

"It's that new hire. She's a pain in the you-know-what to work with," says Kelley.

"You mean Asha?" asks Mona.

"Yeah. She's working in Brian's department. Started a few months ago and already thinks she should be running the place. Totally entitled. Just because she's got an MBA from Northwestern she thinks she walks on water."

"Yeah, I kind of get that vibe too, although I haven't worked closely with her," Mona responds. "It's a generational thing, I think. Millennials. Too many parents giving their kids participation trophies. I don't do that with my son. It completely ruins them once they get into the workforce."

Mona hears something, turns around, and notices Asha sneaking out of the breakroom through the back entrance.

"Oh, crap! How long was Asha there? What did she hear? Crap, crap, crap!"

+++

"I totally agree," remarks Ed.

"With what?"

"With that whole participation trophy thing. We didn't have that when I was a kid. Makes them soft."

"You mean you don't you feel sorry for Asha, Mr. Bleeding Heart?"

"Nope. Those kids need to learn. Tough love. That's what they need."

"Okay, maybe you and Mona are right," I respond. "But that little scene still looks like a bad case of judgment masquerading as office gossip to me."

"Mona's just speaking her mind."

"She barely knows Asha! The most she's said to her thus far is good morning. Now she's made a mess of this relationship and is going to have to dig herself out of the hole she just created."

"I'm sure it will be fine, Shelley."

"Oh sure, Ed. Until Mona needs something from Asha. Then it's going to be quid pro quo. Trust me. I've been there."

"I bet you have. Hit Play, Shelley."

+++

Back at her desk, Mona looks down at her phone and notices a missed call from her son Jeremy.

"Hi, Mom! Really exciting news! I just found out I got accepted to University of Chicago! I know you said it's too expensive and to look at other options, but I really, really want to go. Let's talk about it later tonight, okay? Love you!"

Mona couldn't help but feel very proud of Jeremy.

"The University of Chicago is nothing to sneeze at after all.

It must have been all my excellent mothering, all those nights

I helped Jeremy with his homework at the kitchen table, all

the science fair projects I helped him design. Let's face it. Bill's hopeless at that kind of thing. Yep, behind every talented kid there's a great mother."

Mona was smiling from ear to ear. And then reality set in.

"Oh my God, how are we ever going to pay for University of Chicago?!"

She thinks about all the times over the years when the college fund conversation got shelved. There were always other pressing things that seemed more important at the time.

"How did we get here so quickly? It always felt like there would be more time.

Why did I say yes to that swimming pool? It's been a money pit from day one.

And did we really need two trips to Disney World? The only thing that's magic about that place is how quickly the money disappears from your pocket."

She looks over at the picture of Jeremy on her desk.

"Poor kid! He'll be devastated if we say he can't go. He's worked so hard."

The words of her mother ring in her ear, "Mona, you and Bill need to start Jeremy's college fund right away or you'll be sorry!"

"Crap! I can't believe I'm about to admit that my mother was right. I hate that! Crap! Crap, crap, crap!"

\+++

"Stanford would have been a much better choice," Ed declares.

"What?"

"Have you seen the weather in Chicago in the winter? No thanks."

"Chicago's a great city, Ed."

"It's not even near the beach."

"You've got Lake Michigan right there!"

"It's not the same."

"Whatever. Thanks for the commentary, Ed."

"Her mother sounds like a real pain in the you-know-what too."

"That's not the point, Ed," I say, biting off every word.

"What is the point, Shelley?"

I take a deep breath, gather all my patience (which isn't much by now) and say quite calmly, "The point, Dear Ed, is that financing Jeremy's college education was obviously a priority that snuck up on the family. And now they've been caught with their proverbial pants down."

"Touché."

"If you know what's important to you, then when you say no, you're actually saying yes to something bigger."

"Okay Miss Obi-Wan Kenobi. By the way, do you mind if I quote you? That line might go down really well back at the monastery."

"Ask Stephen Covey. It's his line."

+++

"Hey Mona, do you have a minute?" asks Wendy.

"Sure. What's up?"

"Why don't we go into my office so we can talk privately?"

"Okay, let me grab a notepad and I'll be right there."

The sinking feeling in the pit of Mona's stomach is back.

> *"Oh no, this isn't good. She only drags someone into the office when it's something bad."*

"Hey, Mona, thanks for taking a minute. Go ahead and take a seat," Wendy says from behind her desk.

Mona sits down silently and waits for what's coming next.

"So how's it working between you and Procurement?"

"What do you mean?"

"How would you describe the relationship?"

"It's fine for the most part. Except for the fact that quite often they miss things and get things wrong, which costs me a lot of time. That can be frustrating sometimes."

"Okay, I understand that. It can often be tricky working with other departments. At times I get frustrated too. However, I just had an email forwarded to me by Melinda, the department head. She mentions that your tone was pretty aggressive in an email earlier today to one of her frontline staff."

"What?!"

"Oh really? I mean, I did send an email to one of the analysts. She keeps asking for the same information. Perhaps I was a bit frustrated in the email. Sorry. But honestly, I wouldn't say I'm aggressive. I think she's just really sensitive."

"There was nothing wrong with that email I sent! Wendy has no clue how incompetent that group is. If only she had to deal with them on a daily basis like I do, she'd feel exactly the same! And I can't believe Melinda had the nerve to call Wendy. I better just get out of here and get back to work before I lose my cool!"

"Thanks for the feedback, Wendy. I'll make sure it doesn't happen again."

++

"Rarrh!" Ed yells. "This office is full of catty women!"

"Catty women? I can't believe you just said that, Ed! I resent that! Plus, you know what? You sound pretty silly when you do your tiger imitation."

"But I'm right, aren't I? Take Melinda. The least she could have done is call Mona herself. Why did she have to get Wendy involved?"

"For once, believe it or not, I actually agree with you. Feedback is better when it's delivered directly and not through an intermediary. However, that's still not the point."

"Mona had every right to get upset about the way that was delivered."

"That's still not the point, Ed. How curious was Mona during this conversation?"

"Huh?"

"How many questions did she ask during the talk with Wendy?"

"Well, technically none. But how could she? She was being accused unfairly."

"Unfair is your opinion, Ed. If Mona had stayed curious, she might have learned a couple of things. First of all, she probably would have figured out she never sent that initial response to Procurement in the first place, that it was still sitting in her draft folder.

Second, she would have gotten a much better understanding of why her email was perceived as aggressive and perhaps realized the importance of taking a breather when she's angry. Instead she's caught up in blame (a mindfulness block by the way) and instead of trying to understand what went wrong, Mona's busy pointing her finger at the analyst for being overly sensitive.

Ed! Are you listening to me?!"

"Uh huh."

"Three, if she had probed Wendy a bit more, she might have gotten some additional information about why Melinda reached out directly to Wendy. Chances are there's something deeper going on here."

"That was three."

191

"Huh?"

"You said she might have learned a couple of things, Shelley. A couple is two. You listed three."

"You are so frustrating! What the . . . Did you just hit me on the back of the head with a Cheeto?"

"Maybe."

"Some mystical mindfulness monk you are! I thought non-violence was supposed to be part of your thing."

"It's over-rated. Hit Play, Shelley."

++

Back in the breakroom, Mona helps herself to another doughnut.

"Well, today's a bad day. I deserve it. Besides, I didn't have time

for lunch with all this nonsense. Tomorrow I'll have a salad."

Another doughnut later, Mona hits Send on the email about the Wright account. Problem finally solved. She breathes a much-needed sigh of relief.

"What a day! And it's still only Wednesday. Friday feels like a

million miles away."

And then Mona looks down at her watch. 6:15.

"Crap! I'll never make it to the restaurant on time now. Crap,

crap, crap! Bill is going to be so pissed. Even more than he was

last time. You know what? He needs to chill out. He's always

making a mountain out of a molehill."

Mona runs to the parking garage, but she can't remember where she's parked.

"Damn it! Where was it? I always say I'm going to remember, but I never do. Who builds these stupid parking garages? Every floor looks the same. No wonder I can't find the car! Crap! I'm going to be SO late. Crap, crap, crap!"

Finally Mona finds the car. As she jumps in, banging her shin on the door, she notices that the inspection is overdue.

"Wow, good thing that cop didn't spot it this morning. Bill told me he was going to take care of that. Do I have to do everything myself?"

She fires off a quick text to Bill while she's driving, telling him she'll be a few minutes late. She looks down and sees the gas light flashing.

"Siri, where's the nearest gas station?"

"Hi, Mona. The nearest gas station is the Shell station on Greystone Street, 1.2 miles away."

When Mona gets there, the station is closed.

"Siri, you're a pain in the ass!"

"You're certainly entitled to that opinion, Mona."

"Wow, even the phone has an attitude now."

++

"I have never understood the point of Siri. Half the time she doesn't even understand my questions. I've never found her very useful."

"Gee, I wonder why Siri doesn't understand your questions, Ed?"

"What?"

"Never mind. So what did you notice in this scene, Ed?"

"Huh? Oh yeah, Mona. I'm thinking she must be feeling full of energy after all those KitKats and doughnuts. What kind were the doughnuts?"

"Chocolate."

"Yum! Did they have sprinkles on top? I really like sprinkles."

"Sure, why not?"

"What kind of filling? Chocolate too?"

"Okay, that's enough, Ed. You're starting to piss me off."

"Well, Shelley, if you want to make this believable, I need details!"

"Let's change the subject. What did you think about her texting and driving?"

"I think that was perfectly acceptable in this fast-paced modern world."

"Are you serious? Didn't you see how she narrowly avoided hitting that school bus?"

"There were barely any kids in it, Shelley."

"Barely any kids? Do you listen to yourself? And what about all the blame she's projecting? (Remember, blame is a mindfulness block.) First the procurement analyst. Now Bill. Seems to me she's caught up in her sad little poor me story."

"Bill deserves it."

"And why is that, Mr. Mystical Mindfulness Monk?"

"Poor Mona has to do it all. She works hard, has to help Jeremy countless times with all his school projects late into the night because Bill's so useless. Not to mention cleaning the house and getting dinner on the table every night takes effort too."

"And why, pray tell, do you assume Mona is responsible for cleaning the house and getting dinner on the table?"

"She's the woman."

"Nice, Ed! I'm going to let that go considering I doubt you run into many women at the monastery."

++

Another gas station later, as Mona is standing there pumping gas, her mind starts to wander.

"How the hell did I wind up here? I just chase my tail around and around and never get anywhere. I hate my boss. I hate my job. Years ago, I wanted to be a teacher. What happened? Why didn't I pursue it?"

It was these disturbing questions that were occupying Dear Mona as she pulled up to the restaurant to meet Bill.

"And another work dinner with his firm. I can't stand some of his colleagues. I hope we don't end up at the same table as

Patricia."

"Hi there. I'm here for the Latham and Brooks dinner."

"Sorry, Ma'am. There's no group here by that name tonight," replies the hostess.

"What do you mean?! My husband's firm has this dinner here every summer. He told me to meet him here at 6:30."

"Do you think he could have meant our downtown location? It's just opened, and it's very popular with our corporate clients."

"Oh crap! Bill is going to be furious! Crap, crap, crap!"

An hour late, Dear Mona finally arrives at Bill's dinner, where she finds him seated next to Patricia. He greets her with a scowl.

"Oh hi, Patricia. So good to see you! What a lovely dress."

"Hi there, Mona. It looks like you managed to spill something on yours. What a shame."

"It's going to be a long night."

+++

"Poor little lamb! Shelley, have you no heart? You didn't have to make Mona cry at the gas station," Ed remarks, wiping his eyes with his buttery, popcorn-smudged hands.

"Wouldn't you cry after a day like this?"

"I'd have hung myself with my meditation beads by now. But what does any of this have to do with mindfulness?"

"Chapter 2, Ed, life intention."

"What about it?"

"Well, Mona obviously didn't have one. If she had, she wouldn't have wound up crying into her gasoline about her lost dreams."

"And I can't believe you sent her to the wrong restaurant."

"I didn't do it, Ed. She did it to herself. If she'd been paying attention instead of fumbling for her car keys, she might have remembered what Bill told her about the new location."

"But she was in a rush!"

"That's exactly my point."

"Next time you forget something, Shelley, I won't be so forgiving."

"There won't be a next time."

"And why is that?"

"This book is finally finished, Ed."

"It is?"

"Yep."

"Are you sure, Shelley?"

"You don't want to go back to the monastery, do you, Ed?"

"It's boring there. And they don't have Cheetos. Or doughnuts."

"I thought you liked it at the monastery. You always talk about how peaceful it is."

"It's the same thing, day in and day out, over and over and over again, kind of like *Groundhog Day*. It's enough to make me tear my hair out, if I had any."

"I know the feeling. Don't worry, Ed, there's hope for you yet. If I learned to stop chasing the mechanical rabbit, you can too."

"Mechanical rabbit?"

"Read the book, Ed."

THE END

Acknowledgments

Firstly, I want to thank my amazing husband Vincent for giving me the space to write this book. I use the word space very mindfully and intentionally – there's not many a gal on this earth that has the opportunity to up and quit her high-paying corporate job to start her own business and write a book. You've offered support when I've asked for it, encouraged me when I was frustrated, and most importantly, never once uttered the phrase, "When is this book thing finally going to make money???"

I'd also like to give a shout out to my amazing focus group contributors, who helped with the title and concepts in this book: Kirsten Miller, Aimee Close, Katie Mehnert, Amanda Summers, Liliya Spinazzola, Michele Setzer, Lena Engel, Kathryn Connor and Marion Wust. Thank you, thank you all – you're an amazing group of talented women, and I am honored to know all of you.

To Joani Nunez, Joyce Cavanaugh and Mike Winters at Hot Yoga Houston. A huge thanks for taking a gamble on a skeptic like me and sending me to teacher training. I think it's fair to say it finally paid off. Kudos for all the work you do to develop the next generation of yogis.

To my local ICF Austin Chapter, thanks for the encouragement from many of you to pursue this goal. It takes a community I have often mused...

To Ty at Motiv8 Fitness, my favorite boot camp instructor. Thanks for kicking my butt and encouraging me to keep going on all my goals. Maybe one day I'll finally be first in the run . . . maybe . . .

To the Institute for Professional Excellence in Coaching (iPEC), I never could have achieved this dream without the tools and techniques I learned in my training. Thanks for all the hard work you do to develop the next generation of coaches.

To my family, particularly my Mom and Dad. You've shown support for this crazy venture and even pretended to be interested in the project. ("How's that mindfulness thing going?") Thanks to you both for giving me the courage and fire to go after my dreams.

To my editor and fellow oddball partner in crime, Carol Chesney Hess, I've found your advice to be invaluable. And who wouldn't love an editor that bends over backwards for her author? No matter what bizarre idea I had, you always answered your phone. (I must admit that surprised me.) Best of luck as you integrate those last few final pieces in your move to South Africa. I can't wait to visit.

And finally to Bijoux Kitty, the animal member of the Pernot household, who has been my fellow writing companion over the last six months. You have given me a much needed distraction from my laptop, although I could have done without chasing all the lizards around the house and cleaning up the dead birds and mice. Meow.

About the Author

Shelley Pernot is a coach and trainer who is dedicated to helping people tap into their inner compass so they can live a life filled with passion and purpose. She works with individuals who are seeking more fulfillment and meaning in their lives, as well as with leaders who wish to motivate and inspire their teams to create amazing results. She has learned the importance of these things the hard way, by blindly following a career path that didn't suit her and making loads of embarrassing mistakes along the way. She eventually came to the conclusion that life is too short for things to be just okay.

Shelley is passionate about the topic of mindfulness, so much so that she has dubbed herself the Irreverent Guru of Mindfulness and integrates the practices into the work she does as a coach and trainer. Her vision is to bring mindfulness into the mainstream, and she regularly facilitates mindfulness workshops for busy professionals through organizations such as the University of Texas Professional Development Center.

She is also a certified yoga teacher, a hiker who enjoys being outside as much as possible, and an international woman of mystery who lives in beautiful Austin, Texas with her amazing husband Vincent and kitty Bijoux, the master killer of the lizard population of Travis County. Shelley also loves to think she can sing karaoke and has a knack for killing plants.

Her company is True North Coaching and Development. Check out www.truenorthlifecoach.com for life and career change coaching and www.truenorthdevelop.com for leadership development solutions.

You can contact her at shelley@truenorthdevelop.com.

48419564R00132

Made in the USA
San Bernardino, CA
25 April 2017